Let's Paint with the Master Artist

Dorothy Slikker

Let's Paint with the Master Artist

ReadersMagnet, LLC

Foreword

What are my thoughts and why am I writing this book? I want to show you how and why I paint in the manner that I do. I love the brightness and glow that comes with the Robert Warren's method of painting.

Using an under painting such as the Luminous Orange and the black study is creating a method the old masters used to use. This is called grisaille, a term used in art, painting black and white or complete work done in different shades of gray. Robert did an extensive study of the old masters technique and found that they had created an inner glow in their work. Upon studying their technique he discovered the glow came from underneath the painting. This made him develop his Luminous Orange and with this he created a glow that is so hard not to make you fall in love with his work. The paintings have such a unique quality to them; it makes you guess how he has managed to be so vibrant with his colors and how he maintains a theme throughout the whole piece of work. In most of his paintings Robert uses his Luminous Orange; in his portraits he uses his portrait green to cover his canvas. One of the under color that artist use is a light tan.

I discovered Robert Warren and his paintings on the floor of the Las Vegas Creative Painting Convention. I was so enamored by his work that I knew that was what I wanted my work to look like. I had not at this point taken a class from Robert, but I was ready to sign up for his certification class, that was held in Ohio. I came home all excited and told John all about meeting this fantastic artist and that he had a certification program and I would like to take it. Honey its' in Canal Winchester, Ohio and you have to go for a total of three years. Do you think I could do this? He agreed and I was on my path to my future.

WELCOME WORLD

Teaching and becoming a Master Artist. Becoming a Master Artist opened the doors for me to start writing my first book.

MY ART WALK to the CONTEMPORARY MASTERS this lead to LOOKING BACK THROUGH the life of the MASTER ARTIST and now LET'S PAINT WITH THE MASTER

Dorothy Slikker

Dedication

I want to dedicate this book foremost to my husband of 57 wonderful years. John W. Slikker Jr. has been my best friend and confidant all these years. He has supported all of my endivers even when they fell short of my expectations. A lot of them did not bring me the money that I had envisioned for my life, but I knew John was waiting patiently in the wings of my life. He helped me when I wanted to go to work and started the dress shop by taking over raising the kids on a daily bases. He was a fantastic husband, provider, father and friend all this time.

If you will notice the frames are all alike on my paintings, when I couldn't find what it was that I wanted to show my work in, again John stepped up to the plate and created the look I wanted in my frames. Again he was my life saver.

Doris Smith I would like to bestow upon you all of my gratitude for being my artist friend. Doris is the one that introduced me to so many different art teachers and drug me all over the state to paint with the Jenkins, Johnnie Lillidahl, Bill Bayer and Robert Warren. Doris got me to the Las Vegas Painting Convention and into the classes of some of the most sought after teachers.

Lenora Danielson was my student that had never picked up a brush in her life time. She wanted to learn how to paint, so that she could have something to do in her retirement. She has been so busy painting and crafting that she no longer has time to retire!!!

I really do appreciate all of the students that I have had a chance to touch their lives in some way. I hope that I have had the ability to instill the desire to paint and enjoy themselves with the projects they create.

Why do I paint? I paint for the joy of creating something new and I love to see the looks on people's faces when they see it for the first time.

ENJOY YOUR ART

Lenora's Letter To Dorothy

As a student of Dorothy's I must begin by saying that she has the patience of a Saint. To teach me how to paint was a huge undertaking on her part.

When I first met Dorothy she was teaching art to 5-10 years olds. I asked if I could sit in on her classes. I wanted to learn to paint so bad that I didn't mind sitting in a tiny chair around a tiny round table. She kind of laughed and probably thought to herself "is this woman for real?". Anyway she offered to let me come to her studio and see her work. Which I did. She literally opened Pandora's Box. I knew I had to learn to paint.

For the next 3 years I went to her studio faithfully every week. She began by teaching me the basics in color shadowing and composition. Mind you she had her work cut out for her I had never picked up a paint brush in my life before this.

As the weeks went by I realized that through Dorothy's patience and skilful knowledge, I was learning to paint and gaining confidence in my work.

As with any new learning experience there were a couple rough spots where she had to virtually hold my hand in order to get me to do a proper brush technique. Then there was another time she smacked my arm (in fun of coarse) because I did just the opposite of what she had shown me.

After 3 years I was unable to continue lessons, but with Dorothy's prompting and guidance I knew I was ready to do it on my own.

As I look back on those 3 years I see that through Dorothy's knowledge and talent, she shaped and moulded me into the artist that I am today. For that I will forever grateful. I will always look at the world in a different way.

Since then I have won many ribbons for my paintings, displayed and sold in many galleries and even opened my own Art and Gift shop.

I still call on Dorothy now and then for help with a painting or to get her advice. I can e-mail a picture of my painting to her and she will critique it and always be honest with me—good or bad.

Thank you Dorothy Slikker, for opening up a new and exciting world for me.

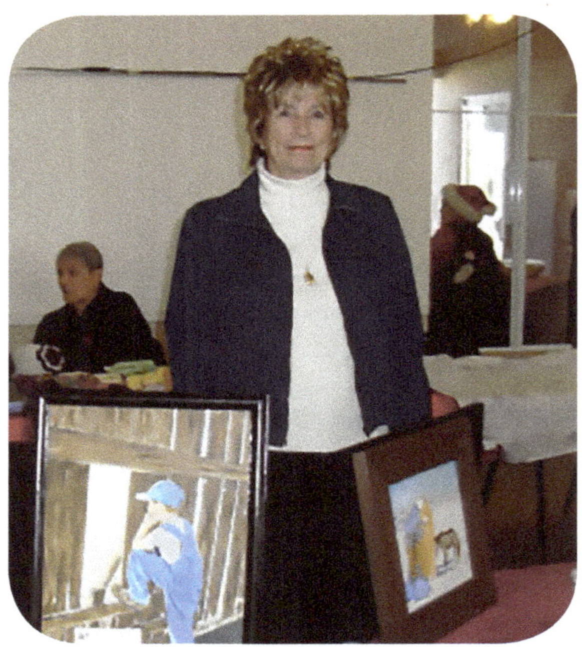

Lenora

Ok Let's Paint

Color Wheel

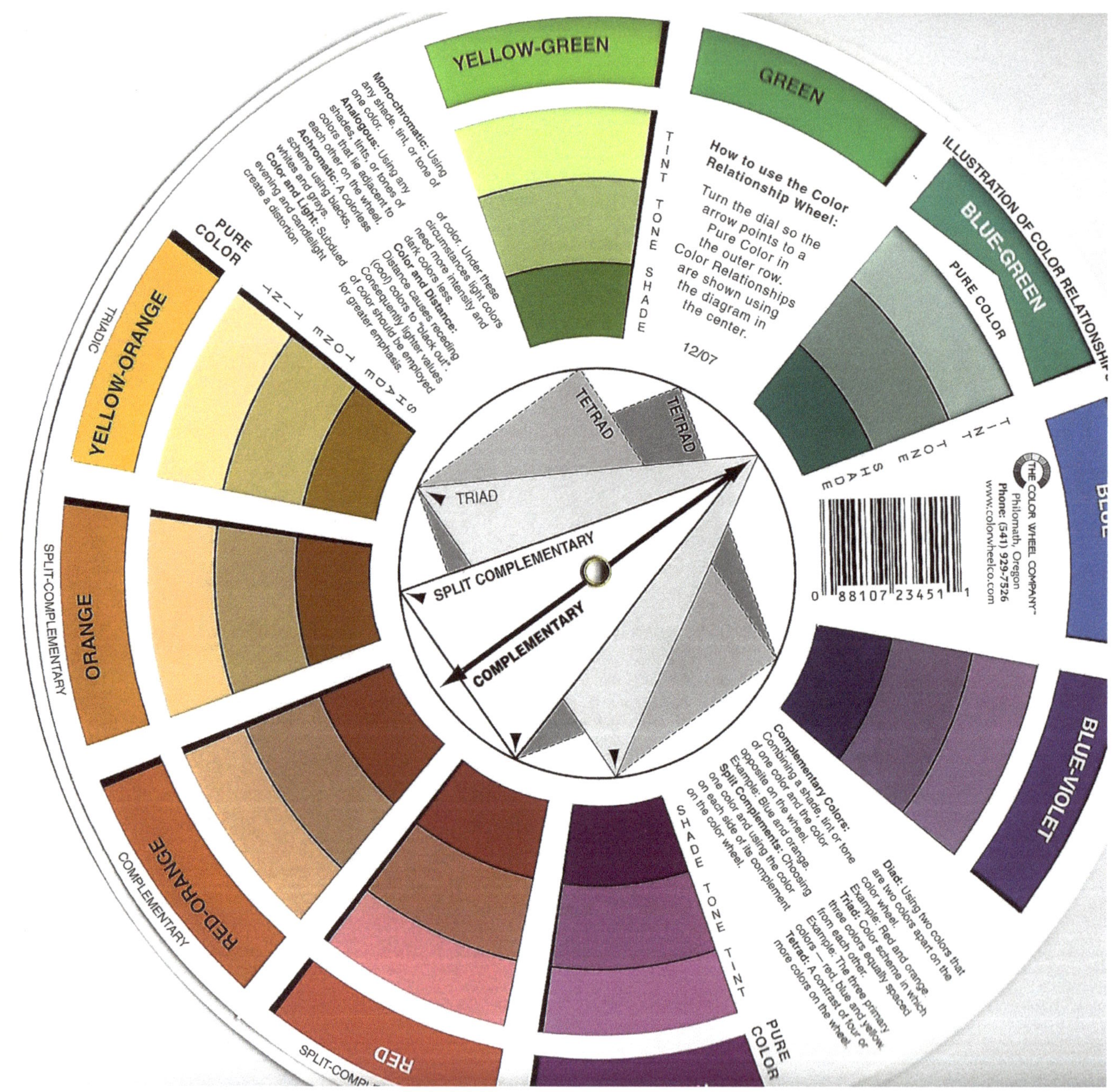

YELLOW-GREEN
GREEN
ILLUSTRATION OF COLOR RELATIONSHIPS
BLUE-GREEN
BLUE-VIOLET
BLUE
RED
RED-ORANGE
ORANGE
YELLOW-ORANGE
PURE COLOR
TINT
TONE
SHADE
TRIADIC
SPLIT-COMPLEMENTARY
COMPLEMENTARY
SPLIT-COMPLEMENTARY
PURE COLOR
TINT TONE SHADE
SHADE TONE TINT
PURE COLOR

TRIAD
TETRAD
TETRAD
SPLIT COMPLEMENTARY
COMPLEMENTARY

How to use the Color Relationship Wheel:
Turn the dial so the arrow points to a Pure Color in the outer row. Color Relationships are shown using the diagram in the center.

12/07

Mono-chromatic: Using any shade, tint, or tone of one color.
Analogous: Using shades, tints, or tones of colors that lie adjacent to each other on the wheel.
Achromatic: A colorless scheme using blacks, whites and grays. Subdued Color and Light: Subdued evening and candlelight create a distortion of color. Under these circumstances light colors need more intensity and dark colors less.
Color and Distance: Distance causes receding (cool) colors to "black out". Consequently lighter values of color should be employed for greater emphasis.

Complementary Colors: Combining a shade, tint or tone of one color and the color opposite on the wheel.
Example: Blue and orange.
Split Complements: Choosing one color and using the color on each side of its complement on the color wheel.
Diad: Using two colors that are two colors apart on the color wheel.
Triad: Color scheme in which three colors equally spaced from each other.
Example: The three primary colors — red, blue and yellow.
Tetrad: A contrast of four or more colors on the wheel.

THE COLOR WHEEL COMPANY™
Philomath, Oregon
Phone: (541) 929-7526
www.colorwheelco.com

0 88107 23451 1

A GUIDE TO MIXING COLOR:

How to use color wheel: Select a color on the outside wheel align it with a color on the inside wheel. The mixture appears in the window.

COLOR DEFINITIONS:

PRIMARY COLORS: Red, yellow and blue cannot be mixed from any other colors.

SECONDARY COLORS: Two primary colors mixed together resulting in orange, green and violet

TERTIARY (INTERMEDIATE) COLORS. One primary and one secondary mixed together.

AGGRESSIVE (WARM) COLORS: Reds, oranges and yellows.

RECEDING (COOL) COLORS: Greens, blues and violets.

1) **Hue: Another name for color**
2) **Tint: color + white**
3) **Tone: color + gray**
4) **Shade: color + black**
5) **Key color: Dominant color in a color scheme or mixture**
6) **Neutral gray: Combination of black and white**
7) **Intensity or chroma: The brightness or dullness of a color**
8) **Value: The lightness or darkness of a color.**

HOW TO USE THE COLOR RELATIONSHIP WHEEL

Turn the dial so the arrow points to a pure color in the outer row. Color relationships are shown using the diagram in the center.

COMPLEMENTAR COLORS: Combining a shade, tint or tone of one color and the color opposite on the wheel. Example: Blue and orange.

SPLIT COMPLEMENTS: Choosing one color and using the color on each side of it complement on the color wheel

DIAD: Using two colors that are two colors apart on the color wheel: Example: Red and orange.

Triad: Color scheme in which three colors equally spaced from each other. Example: The three primary colors_ red, blue and yellow

Tetrad: A contrast of four or more colors on the wheel.

Mono-chromatic: Using any shade, tint, or tone of one color.

Analogous: Using any shades, tints, or tones of colors that lie adjacent to each other on the wheel.

Achromatic: A colorless scheme using blacks, whites and grays.

Color and light: Subdued evening and candlelight create a distortion of color. Under these circumstances light colors need more intensity and dark colors less.

Color and distance: Distance causes receding (cool) colors to "black out". Consequently lighter values of color should be employed for greater emphasis.

Now since I have been saying that I can teach you all of the principles of painting the way I paint, let's get started. One of the first questions that comes to mind is why do you want to paint? Is it because you feel creative, or is it because someone else wants you to? Or are you board and want to try something new to fill your hours during your retirement. All of these reasons are good ones except for the one that someone else wants me to. Art is a very good vehicle to keep the mind and body in sync with the outside world. You become very oblivious of all the things around you and start seeing things as light and dark, shadows. Colors become so prominent in your world.

One of the first things you need to do is to decide what subjects you would like to paint as different things require a different type of canvas.

If for instance you wanted to paint scenery (which is basic) in art, it would require a canvas not a smooth linen, which is used for portraits. This can all come a little later in the class.

Next is picking out your medium oils, water, acrylic, chalk, pencil, or ink. These are some of the things that will determine your choice of canvas or paper. The very most important is the tools you choose to work with. Keeping in mind that the tools are what will make it easier or harder to reach your goal or helping you to be satisfied with your work. As I have stated in my art book or you have seen it on my website a piece of art is only a canvas (with my heart and soul) on it, if you have chosen mediocre brushes then you can expect it to take more out of you than if you have used the good brushes that make the task much easier. This I will bring up again when we get involved in doing a class. The most important thing of all is picking a teacher or mentor that you can build a bond with, someone that is all inspiring to you.

The very next thing that people want to say is that they feel inferior about their ability to draw. Drawing is one of the things I don't brag about as I feel I have no ability in this area. I would tell this person that you can still be an artist, just take photos of the things or subjects you find inspiring to you. If you love it someone else will too. Take the photos of your subject put the photo on your computer and print it in black and white. Now looking at the photo pick out all of the darkest areas of the photo, these are considered your shadows, the lightest of the dark you paint just the nubs on the canvas making it a light gray black. You have now just set the lights and darks in the painting making all the shadows and angles. The next step would be to prep the canvas with Robert Warrens medium, this step allows your paint to be moved around quite easily. Now comes adding your colors, you should have created your first masterpiece.

NOW THE BASICS

Ok we have now decided on our subject, choosing landscape. We have picked our canvas and decided to use a 12″x16″ canvas, I'm choosing to teach the way I got my certification from Robert Warren, so you will cover the canvas with a soft orange acrylic paint and let it dry. Our next step will be to draw or trace our subject. The landscape I chose was a path through the mountains in the snow. Now I would like to ask you what the color of the snow is. Most of you will say blue as this is the way it shows in the photo. Next question is what is the color of water? You will more than likely answer clear. If snow is frozen water why are we painting it blue? Water in the lake or snow on the hill gets its color from the reflections above and around it.

Now before we start to paint let's take a short lesson about placing the points of interest in the right spot on the canvas. I would like to have you mark your canvas lightly with a pencil into three even lines across the top of your canvas and then do the same down both sides and the bottom, you now have divided your canvas in to squares. Looking at the canvas and photo you will see that the clouds start at the top right hand of the canvas reaching the top of the canvas and dropping down to the top and behind the trees. The path or road starts at the same point in the bottom right hand corner. The opposite side of the canvas the line starts on and angle to meet the road line. The fence posts look like they recede into the road getting smaller all the time. This is created by making the fence post all the same height on the top of the post and making it shorter on the bottom, this is the same theory for people on the beach. Another point that I must express is to never paint the land and sky where they are started directly in the middle of the canvas. The land mass must always be above or below the center of the canvas. With this painting you are going to learn about depth perception, point of interest and direct and indirect lighting. Before we begin our project let's look at some drawings that need to be addressed, with these drawings you will learn how to draw some rocks and trees. Another thing to observe is the correct way to hold a brush in order to make it accomplish some of the amazing ways to create a tree and its leaves. Since this painting shows a lot of clouds I am including drawings for clouds, it will show you the proper way to align clouds, one cardinal rule is to never make just odd number clouds do not make three clouds the same and in a straight line. Be fluffy and full, in other words have fun dancing in the clouds.

ROBERT WARREN'S ART LOFT

75 N. HIGH STREET

CANAL WINCHESTER, OH. 43110

614 833 1033

WWW.ROBERTWARRENARTLOFT.COM

INSTRUCTED BY:

DOROTHY SLIKKER

WWW.SLIKKERSFINEART.COM

PAINTS: Weber Prima Oils and Permalba White

White	1″	**Cobalt Violet** ¼″
Cobalt Blue	1″	**Burnt Umber** ½″

Medium: Robert Warren's Professional Clear Medium

Acrylic: Luminous Orange

Brushes: 1″ Brush (to apply medium) cheep as you can find at a hardware store

Palette Knife (for mixing) Fan Brush

#10 Stiff Bristle Brush Hake Brush (soft blender)

Note: Paint should be measured by slicing from a full round bead of paint as it comes from the tube.

CANVAS PREPARTION: With a foam brush apply Luminous Orange wash to canvas and allow for it to dry. Transfer sketch to canvas using gray transfer paper. Using a 1″ applicator brush, generously apply Professional Clear Medium (Canvas should have a solid shine.) Place one paper towel sheet on canvas and over stroke with the brush to pick up excess medium. Reposition the paper towel until you have "brushed over" the entire canvas. This will result in an even satin sheen with no heavy wet areas.

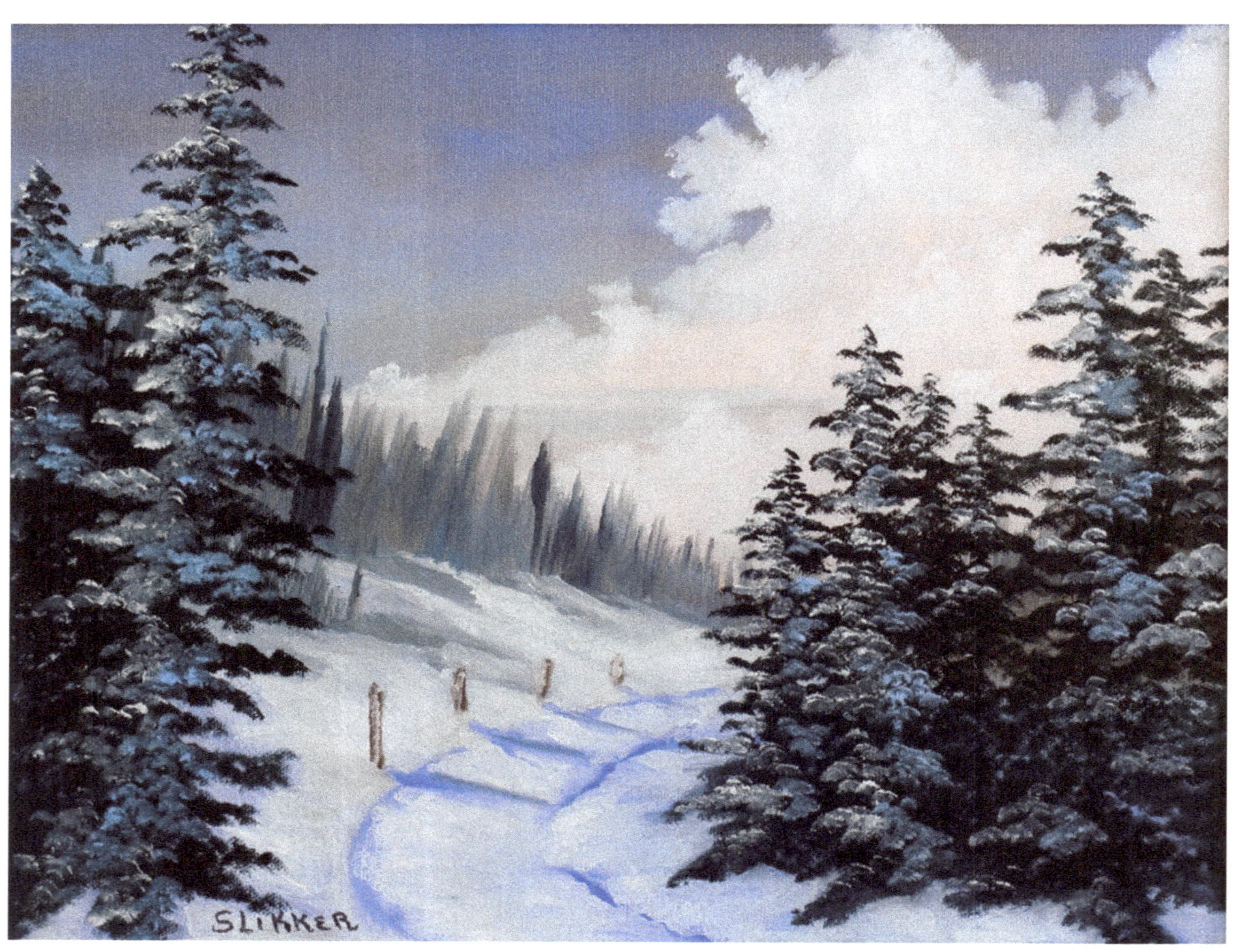
SLIKKER

PRIMA OIL COLOR MIXES:

1) **DARK BLUE** (¼″ Cobalt Blue, ¼″ Cobalt Violet, ⅛ White)

2) **LIGHT BLUE** (¼″ white, ⅛″ Cobalt Blue)

3) **Dark Green** (½″ Cobalt Blue, ½″ Burnt Umber)

#1. Sky and Foreground (#10 stiff Bristle Brush)

  A. **Dark Blue**—Apply across top of canvas working down approximately 4 inches.

  B. **Light Blue—Establish a meadow line across canvas measuring up from the bottom of the canvas. (2-3″** from the bottom middle, 4″ from the bottom on the left) Butt against upper Dark Blue sky area, transition down to the meadow line with a lighter value. Overlap and blend medium value of blue across the width of sky in a 2-3″ layer or band of color.

  C. **Dark Blue**—Add foreground. Transition from a darker value at the bottom to a lighter value at the meadow line. In 2″ blending rows, use an "x" stroke to blend different layer or values together Redefine road edges by adding light blue to the upper half of meadow and road. Maintain dark edges of road.

#2 CLOUDS (Stiff Bristle Brush)

  A. **WHITE**—Control shape and size of clouds. Add the top shape with bright white. Allow middle values to show through the body of the cloud. Slightly overwork bottom of clouds and add a distant impression to lower sky.

  B. **With hake brush mop sky and clouds.**

#3 DISTANT HILL AND TREE IMPRESSIONS (STIFF BRISTLE BRUSH)

  A. **BLUE GRAY** (Brush mix the ¼″ Dark Blue Mix ⅛″ Dark Green Mix and ⅛″ White) Define top shape of distant hill and thinly pull down to slope of meadow. Use a palette knife to shield meadow. Use a vertical edge (1″ up and down scrub) to suggest distant pine trees.

#4 CLOSE PINE TREES (fan brush)

  A. **Dark Green Mix**—Add 5 or more close pines on the right and one large tree on the left with different height tops and varying bottom levels.

  B. **WHITE**—Clean Dark Green Mix from brush and load with White paint. To the sunny side of the tree, add white snow

  C. **LIGHT BLUE MIX**—Very loosely add shadowed snow to the right sides of larger pines. Add a few strokes to the ground. Add bumps to road and slopes.

D. WHITE—Add snow highlight to foreground by dragging and rolling on highlight in the direction of ground. Horizontally blend out any bottom edges or lines into distant tree and add slight impressions of slopes.

E. With the hake brush mop ground.

F. POST—Using your burnt umber add fence post making all the tops level only making the bottoms shorter than the one in front of it and then adding snow to bury them.

I hope you enjoyed doing your first painting with me.

Now that you have finished doing your first painting with me, here are a few questions for your mind to ponder as you look at your masterpiece. Does your painting have:

1. Unequal divisions of space?

2. Small, medium and large areas.

3. Interesting oblique (angled) and interlocking shapes (like puzzle pieces)?

4. Values that can be read from across the street?

5. A center of interest? Do the darkest darks, lightest light, line direction and riches color lead your eye to a focal point?

6. A pattern of interesting multi-shaped darks?

7. An interesting pattern of highlights?

8. Many graduations or transitions of values or blended areas of color?

9. An area of detail referred to as lace?

10. Are there some areas left to the imagination? Lost edges or impression?

Dominance in the 7 elements of design?

1. Line

2. Value

3. Color

4. Texture

5. Shape

6. Size

7. Direction

   A. Symbols of strokes or shapes that suggest or express what the painting is communicating.

   B. Creativity and/or originality. Is subject matter handled in an original or creative matter?

   C. Impact! Does it elicit a strong or immediate response or mood?

Taken from Robert Warren's information.

Painting Notes

1. Cool colors recede
2. Warm colors advance
3. Distant colors are dull with a haze of atmosphere)
4. Close colors are rich or more intense
5. Dark values get lighter in the distance
6. Clouds are flatter near the horizon
7. Waves are flatter near the horizon
8. Rocks have flat bottoms near the horizon
9. In clear water, the reflections are darker than the real objects
10. In murky water, the objects reflect lighter
11. Rocks have many planes and angles
12. Paint layers of low distant clouds before closer and higher overlapping clouds.
13. Don't let highlights escape the edges of the canvas
14. Don't direct a line to the corner of the canvas
15. Don't highlight everything equally
16. Stay well enough organized to achieve your goals (Ex Finish 1 painting a week.
17. Don't let too much organization slow you down (No excuses)
18. Ignore the "dream breaker" or negative people
19. Ask advise from people who know
20. Create either high key (more light) or low key (more darks) paintings, but not an equal balance of lights and darks.
21. Don't knock the life out of a painting by overworking
22. Always think small, medium and large for every subject, but not in that order
23. Abstracts are like a song without words
24. Values create dimension
25. Values do all the work and color gets all the credit
26. Contrast lights and darks, but just as importantly contrast temperatures of colors
27. Intuition in art is actually the result of prolonged tuition
28. The amateur is afraid of boldness, the professional is afraid of timidity
29. One reward for sketching is learning to see.
30. We are not artists, but entertainers
31. Give me a student who is will to work hard rather than someone depending on talent.

Robert Warren

I learned from Robert that there are 8 principles of design

Unity	Alternation
Conflict	Balance
Dominance	Harmony
Repetition	Gradation

Elements of Design

Line	Shape
Value	Size
Color	Direction
Texture	

Robert Warren

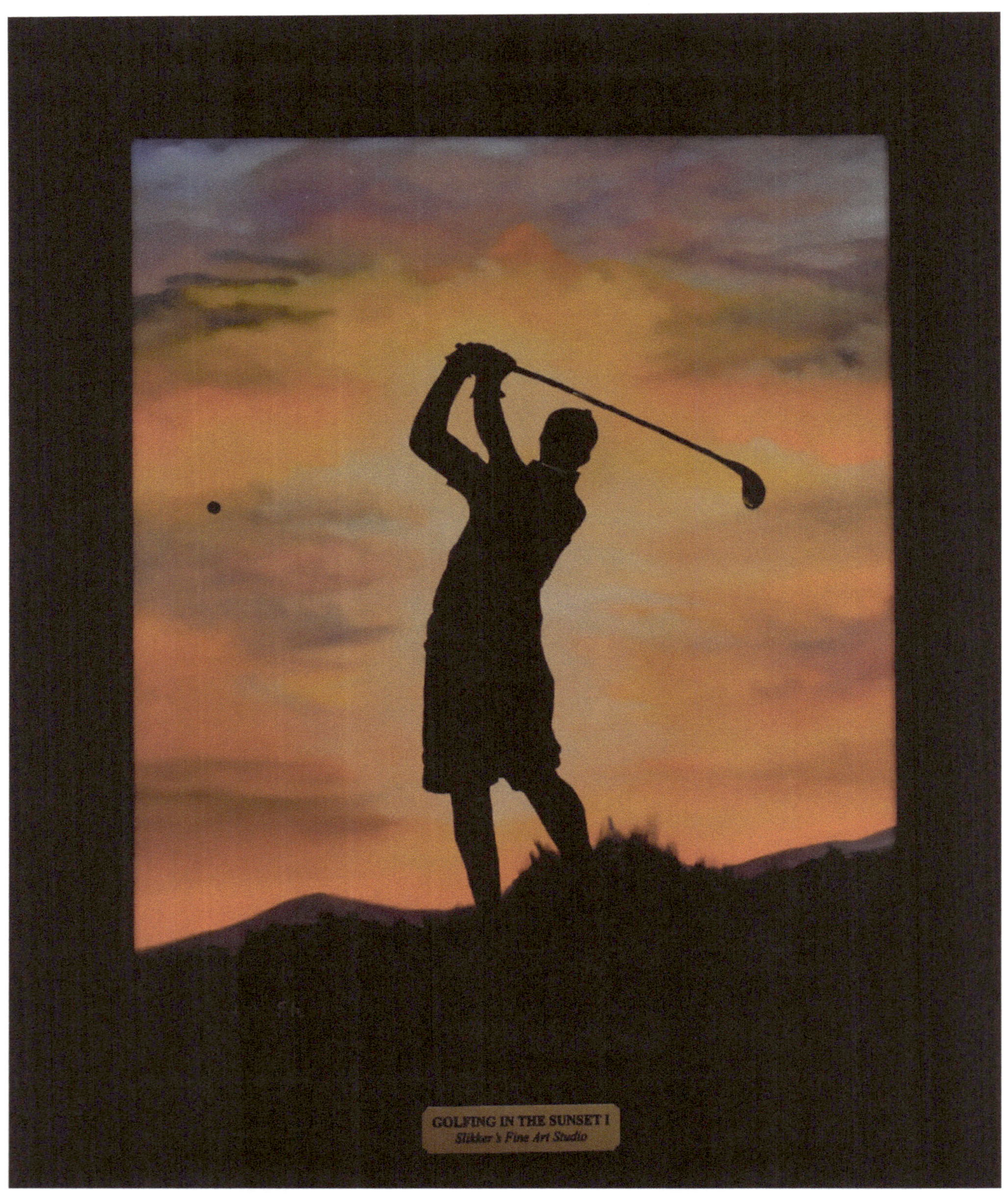

THE GOLFER
www.slikkersfineart.com

COLORS:

1. French Ultramarine Blue
2. Alizarin Crimson Permanent
3. Cadmium Yellow Med.
4. Cadmium Yellow Light
5. Cadmium Orange
6. Lamp Black
7. Titanium White
8. Prima Peach

Preparation of the Canvas: Cover the entire canvas with Robert Warren's Luminous Orange, and then applies the pattern after the orange has dried using black graphite paper. Next paint the pattern using the black and white picture as a guide for the dark and gray application of Grumbacher's Mars Black Hue Acrylic. After the paint is dry (only a few min.) cover the entire canvas with Robert Warren's Professional Clear Medium and laying a paper towel on canvas, stroke with a 1″ brush, leaving it moist enough to see your finger print when you touch the med.

Almost always I mix my colors with the brush or the canvas (which we will do today)

NOW LET'S PAINT

I always start at the top of my canvas and work my way to the bottom (note never put land in the center of the canvas. My rule of thumb is dividing your canvas into thirds and places the land mass above or below the middle of the canvas.

SKY: The sunset starting at the top. I usually start in the right and left hand corner of the canvas going across the top with the French Ultramarine, as you work your way down the canvas blend Alizarin Crimson and white. On your way down the picture blend in the Orange and the two yellow (Cad Med & light) forming a halo around the golfer, going all the way to the land mass, in the center of the halo and around the golfer using the Prima Peach to complete the glow in the halo, all the while using the soft brush for blending and smoothing the effect. That would be your Hake Brush.

GOLFER: Paint the entire golfer with lamp black. Where the folds are in the golfers clothes high light with the lavender. At the same time high light the gloves and hat. Also at this time you need to add the ball in the distance. Also highlight the golf club that you painted with the golfer.

FIRST HILLS: Paint the hill with the mixture of French Ultramarine Blue and Alizarin Crimson and white, making a light hill in the distance.

GOLF COURSE: Paint the entire hill with Lamp Black and highlight with Alizarin Crimson and White. Now let's make the weeds and grass. Paint them with your liner brush with black and highlight with Alizarin Crimson & white.

Walla, Now sign your painting. (Be happy)

NOTE: You did not hear me talk about paint turpentine for cleaning brushes that is because as a Robert Warren Artist we do not use turpentine for cleaning we use Baby Oil. It is non toxic and will not cause lung problems or cause cancer. It cleans up our messes and makes for a healthier artist.

Now take the time to go back to the Critics Sheet and evaluate the progress you are making. Remember you are the one who needs to be happy.

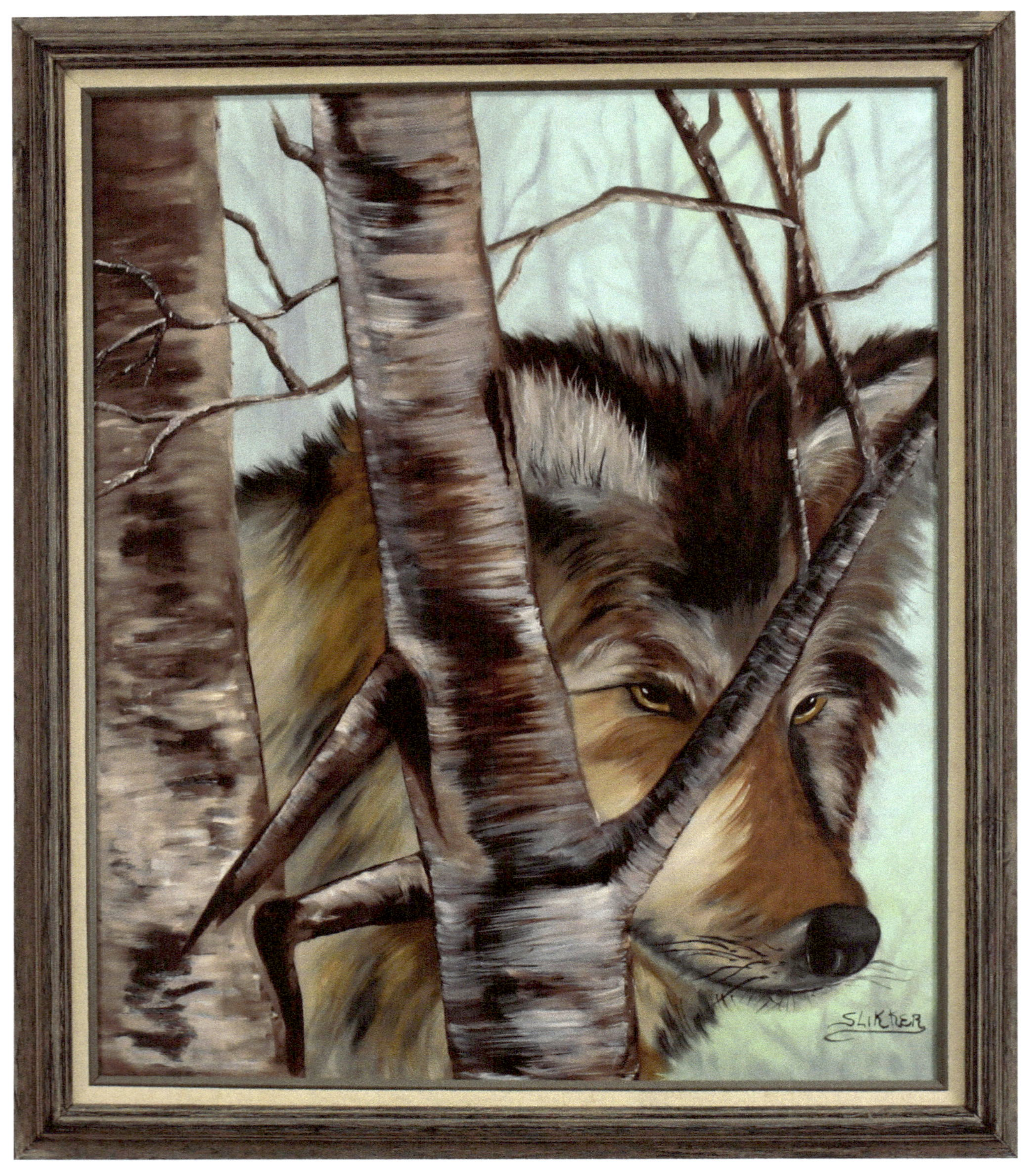

www.slikkersfineart.com
ON GUARD
16″x20″

First you will prep your canvas with a soft gray acrylic paint. The reason for the change from the orange is you are going to try to create a look of mist or fog in the background. After it dries you add your drawing, and then cover the image with the black acrylic using your black and white picture as a reference guide for the application of the black. Cover the entire canvas with the Robert Warren medium using a towel brush over it until you can see the finger print on your hand.

PAINTS:

Turquoise, White, Lamp Black, Burnt Umber, and Raw Umber, Yellow Ocher.

BRUSHES: 1″ cheap bristle bush, 1′4″ or a #2 brush, ½″ brush and a fur brush

Sky: I like to use my bristle brushes for the background as it is easier to push the color around the canvas. Make a mixture of light turquoise a touch of blue (a very small touch). After the sky is finished mix a very light burnt umber and white to put the trees in the fog. You should have painted them black and painted over them with the sky color. This is in case I was not clear at the beginning.

Eyes: I always start with the eyes of an animal or person; this is to set the mood or movement of the painting. Use the #2 brush to paint the line above and around the eye with Lamp Black. Next use the same brush and place the pupil in the eye using the same black. Now use the yellow Ocher and fill in the space between the pupils. The highlight on the pupils should sit on the line of the pupil and the color on each eye in the same place. This will make it look like the animal has his eyes on you all the time.

One thing to remember is that on animals both sides of the face have the same colors in the same place. Now that you have the eyes set into place continue up the face using the colors that you see on the colored picture. Start with the white around the eye as you see it. Then follow with the Burnt Umber softened with white. Going up the face use Burnt umber and black mixed to go between the eyes and ears. The top of the ears also get the darker of these colors. Alternate using umber and white along with yellow ocher and raw sienna. Doing this part of the animal becomes much easier if you use the fur brush.

NOSE OR SNOUT: look at your photo to make the snout come forward away from the face you have to create a shadow between the snout and face do this by using the burnt umber. The top of the snout is created by using raw sienna and some yellow ocher; finish the snout using a light color of yellow ocher or raw sienna, working around the tree branch. Using lamp black for the nose paint the complete nose and come back with some white to flatten the top of the nose curving your brush on down to the bottom of the nose. Now take some of the white and make the curves or circles for the nostril. The mouth should be done at this time softening the black with white making a soft gray. Use this mixture as you see it on the picture. Follow this method of painting until you have covered the entire wolf. Please pay attention to the direction of your brush strokes, this make all the difference in the world.

TREES: Paint the front trees burnt umber, all of the branches and knot holes. Now you are going to put white on your pallet and stretch it thin so that you can run your pallet knife on its side to drag a bead of paint. Using the pallet knife place it on its side and slide it from the right to the left, making sure it has a slight curve to produce the desired effect on the tree. I am not good with a pallet knife so I gave up and used my ½″ brush to make the highlights on the tree and brushes. Learning to paint with a pallet knife is a plus when you want to add a rugged texture, but if you don't master this technique a brush is fine. Remember this is your painting and we are not all alike. Be Happy

After you have finished each painting why don't you sit down and write what it is that you learned new? What did you experience that you had never thought of doing? How do you like doing the black study? Does it help you at all when you are ready to mix and use your paint?

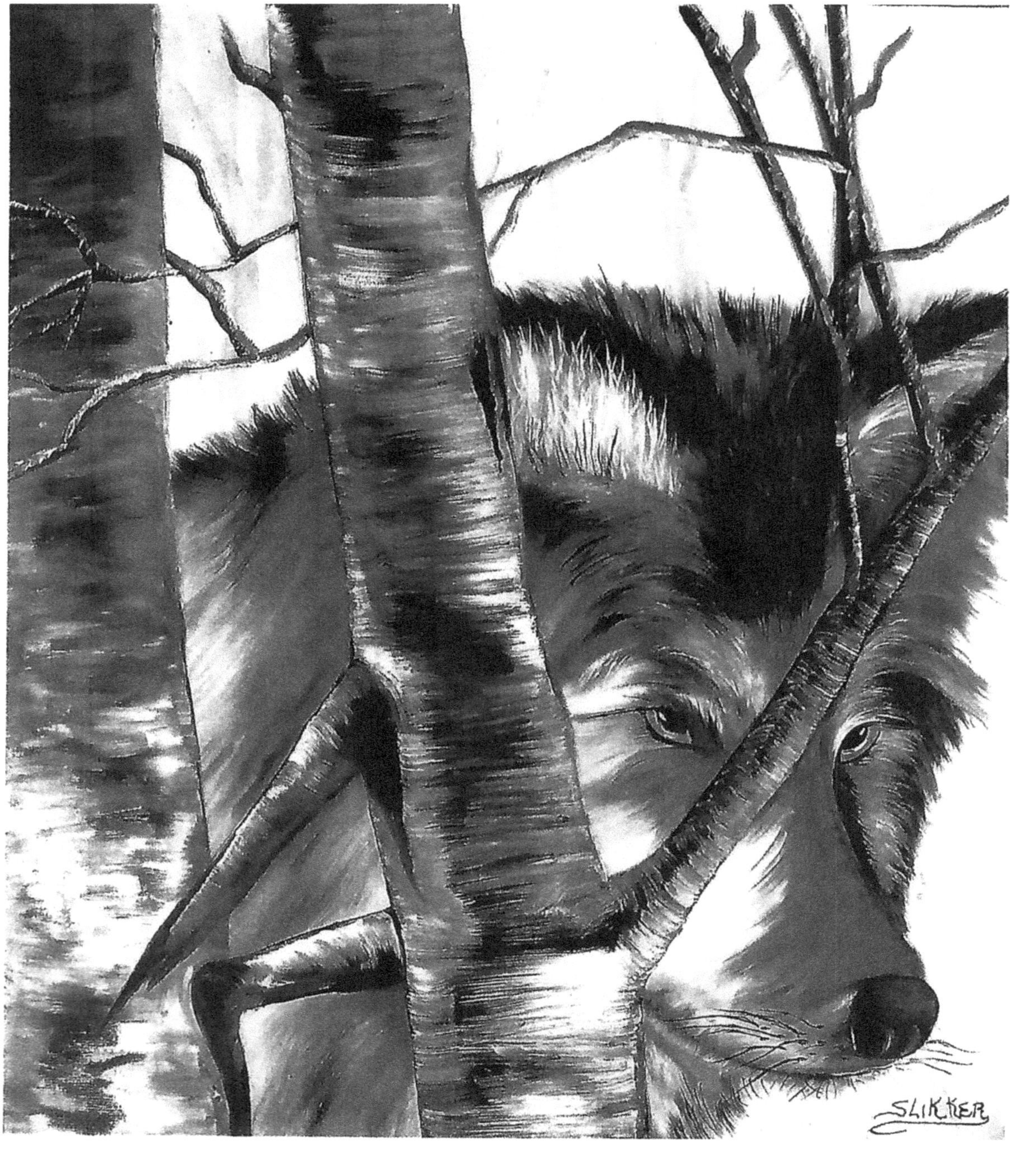

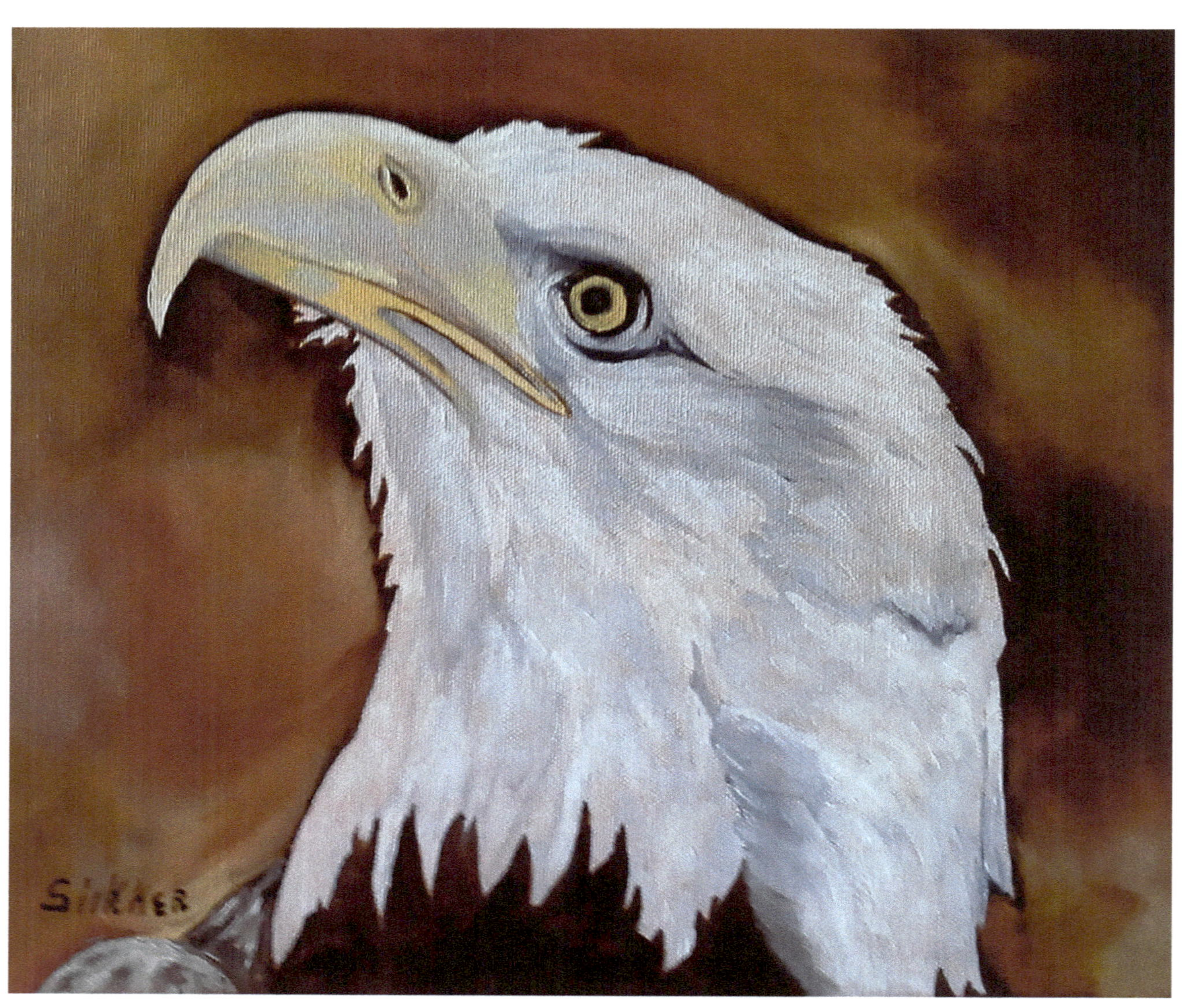

www.slikkersfineart.com
HIS MAJESTY
11″x14″

Painting the eagle is one of my favorites. He is the bird the represents the truth and love of the American People. He is on our money and some of our flags. With the mighty sweep of his wings he encompasses all of us as he flies overhead, no one is left behind. He is our Magical Bird that represents all American's as our National Bird.

Now let's give him life!!!

We shall begin by preparing our canvas using Luminous Orange. We will let it dry for a few minutes. Now we should use a black and white copy of our project and proceed to either trace our eagle or draw it on the prepared canvas. Using the pattern we will proceed to copy the darks and lights in the same manner that I have explained in the other paintings. After a short drying time, it will be the time to use the medium that is from Robert Warren's formula. Others do not work as well. At the end of the book I will add a page so that you will be able to order straight from Robert Warren yourself. At this time you use a paper towel on the canvas and brush over the project until when you touch it you can see the finger print clearly on your finger.

BRUSHES:

I noticed that I did not tell you the brand of brushes I us. "Scharff" is the Co. that I use. I like the soft sable, the soft way it is too paint with. When I use a bristle brush it is also a scharff. Then I deal with only one Co. They are not the cheapest on the market, but they are the best.

½″ bristle brush
½″ sable brush
¼″ sable brush

PAINT:

Burnt umber ½″
Burnt sienna ½″
White 1 ½″
Lamp Black ¼″
Cad. Yellow Light ¼″
Yellow Ocher touch of color

BACKGROUND: Paint the background with you mixture of light and dark Versions of your Burnt Umber using some white to soften, if you desire you can add a little of the Yellow Ocher to give it a spot or two of light.

EYE: Using your ¼″ sable brush draw the black circle around the eye, now using the same brush put in the pupil of the eye define the straight line above the eye, this helps the bird to look more intense and in charge. Using the yellow ocher put in the ring around the pupil. Using some white make a pleasing gray for around the eye and high light with white. Don't forget the sharp line below the eye in black .

HEAD: Using the combination of white and gray feathers paint the head remembering to make the feathers flow the direction of the head. The rule of thumb is always correct light against dark. Remember this when you are making the feathers and you want to acquaint with the division of colors to make some of them to protrude.

BREAST: Now that you are working on the dark feathers under the head using the same strokes as the head paint with the Burnt Umber. As you work on the wing and the small triangle piece use white with the burnt umber. Drop to more White on the top of the one wing, you should have three different values of this same color.

BEAK: Painting the beak we use our cad. Yellow light and cad. Yellow med. The top of the beak will always catch the light so use some white on top of the beak always painting in the forward down motion. As you get closer to the under beak the color becomes darker use some gray and a little brown to darken the under beak. I used some burnt umber to make the beak appear to sit down over the under beak. I also dabble a little of the light gray on the upper beak. Use the black in the nostril on the beak and use some light gray to encase the nostril and high light it with cad. Yellow med.

I hope you enjoyed this project. It makes you notice shadows and blending when you can. With this eagle you need to be aware of the subtle little changes is color, they are not dramatic, but if they are not there it will ruin the effect you want to have. No matter how you try to rid yourself of the orange under painting it will always show through when you paint with the white and blue.

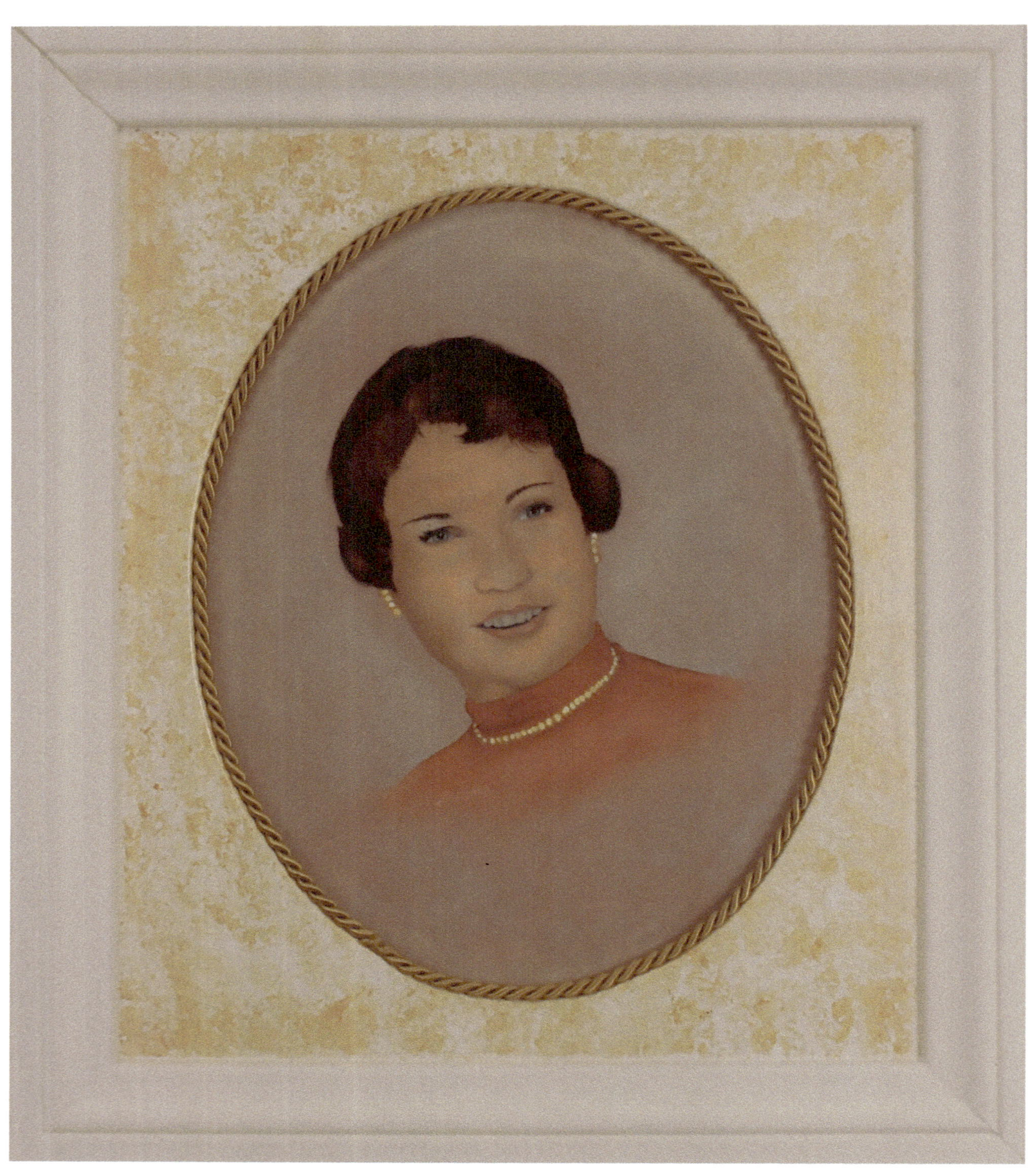

Dorothy Slikker age 17
www.slikkersfineart.com

Today we will paint a portrait. I started with a black and white photo of myself to use for my pattern. When I do a portrait I always trace the subject so that I may capture the look or the moment of the time. Some rules I always go by is to first touch my face and find all the places that have bone right under the skin and the parts of the face that protrude. These areas will always have the lighter tone for the skin. All of the soft tissue will always collect the shadows and is of the darker tone.

When we paint the face if it is of a man it will demand a larger canvas 18″x24″. A woman or child will be on a smaller canvas 16″x20″. The man's head will take all of, or most of the canvas and a woman or child will be dominate in the middle of the canvas. If you are painting a mother and child you need to decide what the moment is about? If you notice on the upcoming reference paper you will be able to see that in the eye there is very little white. Notice that the dark takes over as shadow because the bone above the eye protrudes over the eye ball. You must always keep in mind the shadow in the eye. Remember the eyes always tell the story of the time, place and event that the person is in. Enjoy drawing and practicing doing the different elements of the face.

Let's start by viewing a worksheet of the human head.

When we paint a portrait we use the portrait green to prep the canvas. This is available through Robert Warren's website. The reason that you don't see so many lines on my face in the photo is that I used a small brush laying it flat and moved it in a circular motion, this enabled me to blend as I worked on the face it's self.

CONSTRUCTION STEPS OF AN ADULT FACE:

1. Draw an approximately 6″ circle.

2. Divide with light lines horizontally (this will be the brow line) and vertically through the middle.

3. Establish Eye Line—1/3 Radius below Brow line.

4. Establish Chin—Equal distance from eye level top of head and from eye level to chin mark.

5. Create Egg Shape determining jaw shape. Slice off approximate ¼″ from sides of original 6″ circle.

6. Locate bottom of nose—Equal distance between brown line and chin.

7. Lower Lip—Equal distance between nose and chin, scraped

8. Upper Lip—Equal distance between lower lip and nose line.

9. Hair line—Same distance above brow line as nose is below brow line.

10. Determine—5 equal space across eye line 2½″ spaces on each side of vertical center. (Spaces approximately 1 ⅛th″ each)

11. Nose width equal to eye spaces.

12. Mouth width approximately equal to iris edges.

13. Ears between eye and nose line.

14. Ears between eye and nose line.

15. Hair line variable. Eyebrows on brow line

16. Contour draw features and shade.

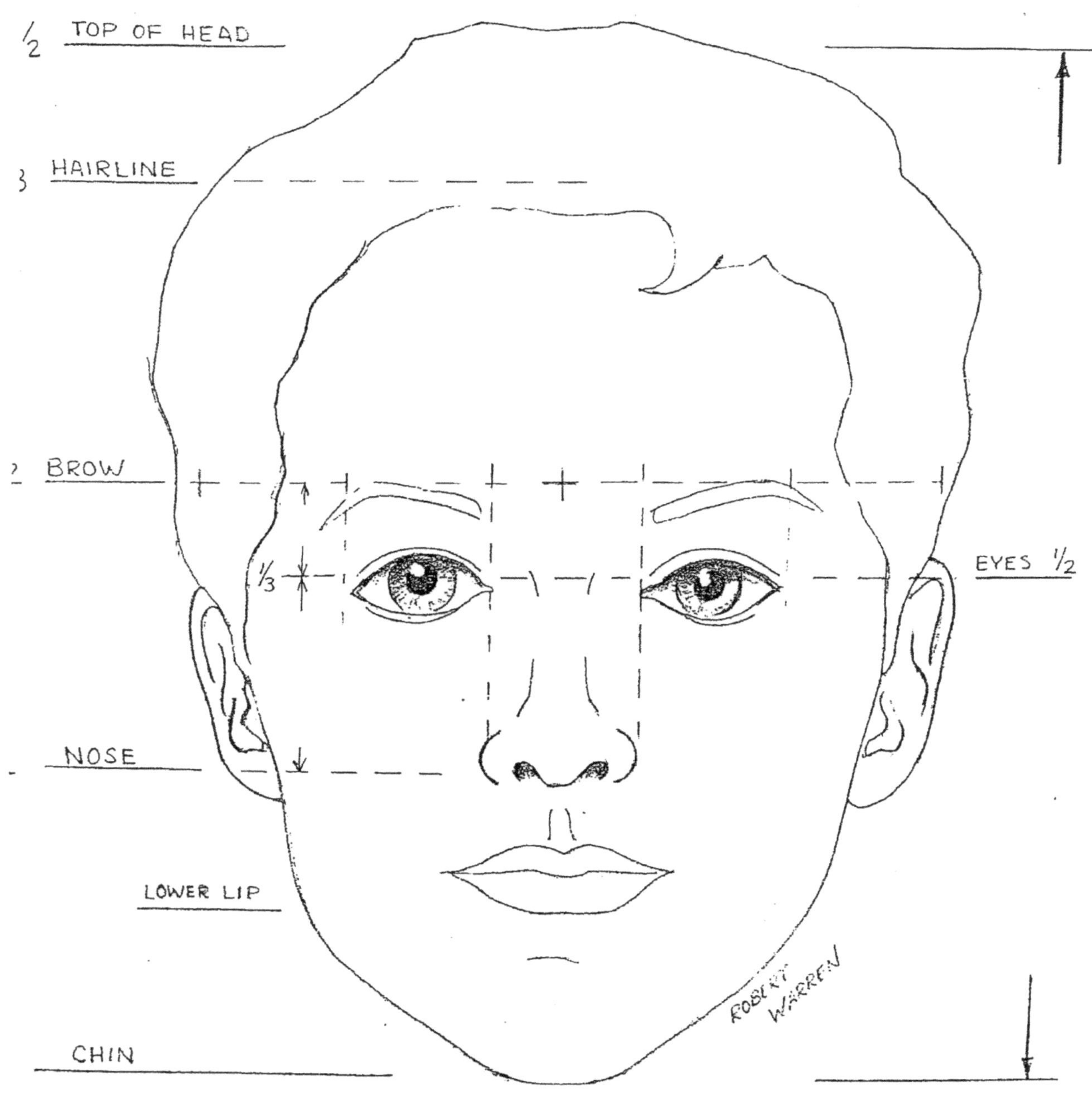

1/2 TOP OF HEAD
3 HAIRLINE
2 BROW
EYES 1/2
1/3
NOSE
LOWER LIP
ROBERT WARREN
CHIN

POSITIONG SUBJECT ON CANVAS:

Use the eyes of your subject as a reference. There are no concrete rules to positioning, but I have always positioned my subjects to look comfortable by using these basic guidelines:

1. An adult male's eye line should be a few inches above the center of the canvas to suggest height.
2. An adult female's eye line should be on or slightly above the center of the canvas.
3. A child's eye line should be below the center of the canvas to suggest smallness.

Using the following outline as a guide, try to sketch the subject with broken, angular lines and even exaggerate if necessary, and the slightest curve or angle change. This is necessary because the later application of oil paint with the brush with convert angles to smoother contours.

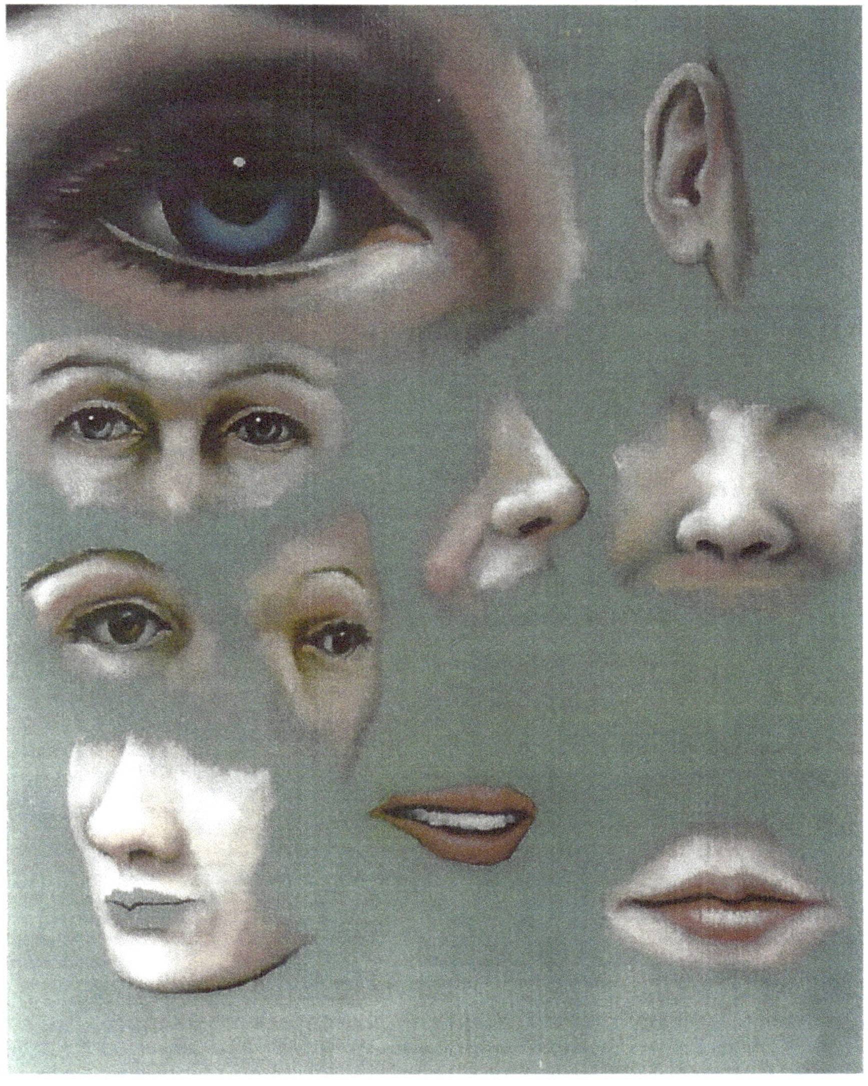

MOST IMPORTANT LINES THAT DETERMINE THE LIKNESS OF THE SUBJECT:

A. EYES:

1. Eyelids—Is there a separate crease line above the upper eyelid? Sketch angles for crease and upper and lower eyelids.

2. Exact location of the iris curves. If guessing, make the curved edges the same in each eye. Indicate perfect circle pupils exactly centered in middle of iris. Check for even distances to outer edge of iris. Define tear duct.

3. If there are many lines and wrinkles, shade with the pencil as you sketch for less confusion later.

4. Sketch eyebrow placement and shape

B. NOSE:

1. Nostril Flairs (outer flairs of nose) can usually can be seen. Keep horizontally parallel with eyes and mouth.

2. Nostrils are generally shaped with 3 or 4 angles or just a slight suggestion.

3. Shade with pencil: the bridge shadows and if seen, sketches the highlight spots on the bridge, ball and/or nostril flairs.

C. MOUTH:

1. Define crease with angles and any defined lip edge. Don't define entire shape unless lipstick is used.

2. Teeth and Gums—Sketch opened angles of the teeth and indicate gum "tapers" at the top of upper teeth. (Occasionally, just dots will work.) Don't make lines between teeth unless there is an obvious gap.

D. FACE LINES:

1. Any definite lines on forehead, around corners of eyes, under eyes, smile of cheek lines, dimples, chin crease, neck lines.

2. Sketch any definite shadow shapes. Example: hair shadows on forehead or shadows around and under nose, under lip and chin, shadow on neck, jaw or cheeks shaped with shadows.

3. Sketch in highlight shapes on forehead, cheeks, nose, lip, chin, neck.

E. OUTER SHAPES:

1. Jaws chin and shape of head if seen.

2. Hair on actual size of subject should be sketched ½″ shorter for loose hair to allow for wispy brush strokes. Define closer outline for baldness, short or tight hair. Shade dark masses in hair and add contours lines in highlight areas.

F. CLOTHES, HANDS, ARMS:

1. Sketch any important lines or patterns of clothes. Shade folds for understanding. Accuracy is important on hands and fingers.

FINAL NOTE—After using the projector, refer to the photograph for the sharper details, but trust your projected lines.

PORTRAIT COLOR MIXES

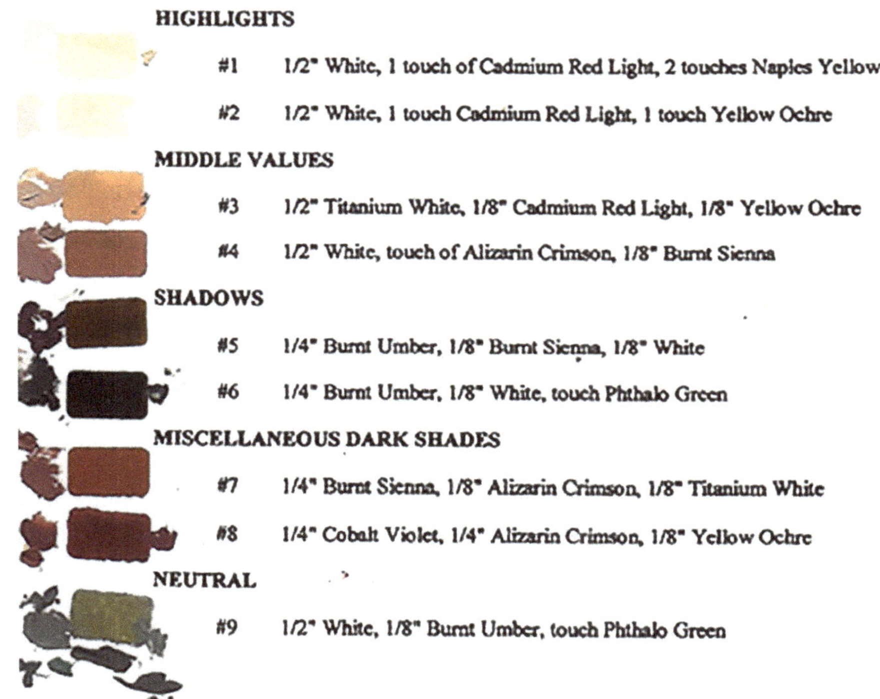

EYES—Use a #4 Badger Filbert or Flat for details.

A Eye Structure—Ivory Black:

With a small brush, define crease of eye, upper eyelid, and pupils. Outline iris and stretch in color toward pupil leaving a crescent highlight area.

B. Eye Color—It is impossible to give definite formulas for eye colors, however, these formulas should give you a base for your own work.

1. **Blue Eyes**—(touch Titanium White and Cobalt Blue) tap in lower half of iris. Wipe out brush and add Yellow Ochre and Titanium White, **tap in crescent highlight.**

2. **Blue Green Eyes**—(touch Titanium White and Cobalt Blue) blend out of upper shadow and tap in lower of iris. Wipe out brush and add a touch of Yellow Ochre and Cobalt Blue and Titanium White. Tap in crescent highlight. Wipe out brush and add Titanium White with just a touch of Yellow Ochre. Highlight crescent shape next to pupil.

3. **HAZEL EYES—(**Touch each titanium White, Cobalt Blue, Flesh Color #9 Neutral) Blend out of upper shadow and tap in lower of iris. Wipe out brush and add a touch of Cobalt Blue Yellow Ochre and Titanium White. Tap in crescent highlights. Wipe out brush and add Titanium White with just a touch of Yellow Ochre. Highlight crescent shape next to pupil.

4. **GREEN EYES**—(touch Yellow Ochre and Cobalt Blue) tap in lower half of iris. Wipe out brush and add Titanium White and Yellow Ochre tap in crescent highlight.

5. **BROWN EYES**—(Burnt Umber) highlight with Burnt Sienna and White.

C. Flesh Color #6 (refer to color chart for flesh) Work out of shadowed corners creating shaded areas of white of eyes.

D. Flesh color #9—Add lighter value to White of eye next to iris.

E. Flesh Color #2—Add a touch to warm whites of eyes. Re-accent and blend again for final and blend into shadow.

F. Ivory Black—Tap down shadow of upper eyelid across iris.

G. White—Add catch light to both eyes at the same point in eye. Add a gray catch light if eyes are in a shadow.

H. Flesh Color #7—Tap in tear duct. Highlight with **Flesh Color #4** and underling flat pink edge of lower eyelid.

2. **FACE LINES** (Small brush)

A. **Flesh Color #6 with touch of Flesh Color #8—Paint in nostril. Add a touch of Ivory Black to darken top half of nostril.**

B. **Flesh Color #8 with touch Flesh Color #6—Add line between lips. For fuller lips, add to lower middle edge.**

3. **Dark Shadows—Flesh Color #6** (Filbert Brush) **For Flesh Areas: it is extremely important to paint shadows very thin or lean and highlights very thick or fat with proportional middle values.**

These are examples only. Adjust areas of shadows to meet the needs of your portrait.

A. Add hair shadow against head and face by loosely outlining hair.

B. Add shadow under chin.

C. Define neck shadows

D. Add shadows around eyes.

E. Define eye sockets and work down to blend around nostril flairs of nose and under nose.

F. Add shadow under nostrils.

G. Add shadow under lower lip.

8. **Extending shadows—Flesh Color #5** (the warmer of the two shadow colors) (Filbert Brush) Wipe out excess paint from brush and apply by extending out of shadows with a transparency to allow blue/green canvas to show through. Add warmer shadows against the dark shadows extending out from darks.

9. **Skin Highlights—Flesh Color #2** (Filbert Brush) Add highlights to forehead, brow, cheeks, and bridge, ball and nostril flairs of nose. Add to upper lip, philtrum, and around mouth.

MIDDLE VALUES:

A. **COOL VALUE—USE Flesh Color #4** (cool) middle value. Add cool middle values against all shadows. Add between shadows and highlights. Add to upper eyelids.

B. **WARMER VALUES—Flesh Color #3** for a more orange (warm) middle value. Work warmer middle values into remaining area while following contours of face. Also add to any small areas between cool middle values and highlights.

7. REFLECTED LIGHT: (COLOR VARIABLE) usually related to color of clothing. (Filbert brush).

Placing in shadows, add a stroke under chin, cheeks, jaw, brow, on nose above nostril, etc. Consider using a glaze of the **Flesh Color #7 or Flesh Color #8** as a bluish under cheek bones, end of nose, and under chin. Also consider these two dark colors in the darkest shadows.

8. LIPS—Natural Color (small brush)

A. **Flesh Color #7—Shadows**

B. **Flesh Color #4—Middle Values**

C. **Flesh Color #2—Highlight**

D. **Flesh Color #8—Restate crease between lips if necessary.**

9. TEETH (small brush)

A. **Flesh Color #6 or Black—add to corners.**

B. **Flesh Color #9—Work out from darks into light.**

C. **Flesh Color #2—Focus on and Highlight each tooth separately.**

D. **Flesh Color #6—Tap shadow down onto upper teeth.**

E. **Flesh Color #1—Accent a final shine to middle teeth.**

10. Gums or tongue.

    A. Use Flesh Color #8 for shadows.

    B. Touch of Cadmium Red Medium for a rich red

    C. Flesh Color #4 for a final highlight.

11. Background (Stiff Bristle Brush stokes) Important to control contrast around subject. Lights around dark areas and darks against light areas. May be mottled or smooth. Generally cool or neutral colors compared to skin.

HAIR:

When painting the hair take note of the color of your photograph, such as the one of myself that I have presented. I used Burnt Sienna, Burnt Umber and Yellow Ocher for highlights.

CLOTHES:

I used a combination of Cadmium Medium Red and Cad. Med. Red Light. I then finished the portrait with the jewelry. Now that the painting has set for awhile and the paint has had time to set I went back and put in the eye brows and eye lashes using the Burnt Umber for the brows and black for the eye lashes.

With the hake brush you can lightly soften the portrait and soften the lines on the face.

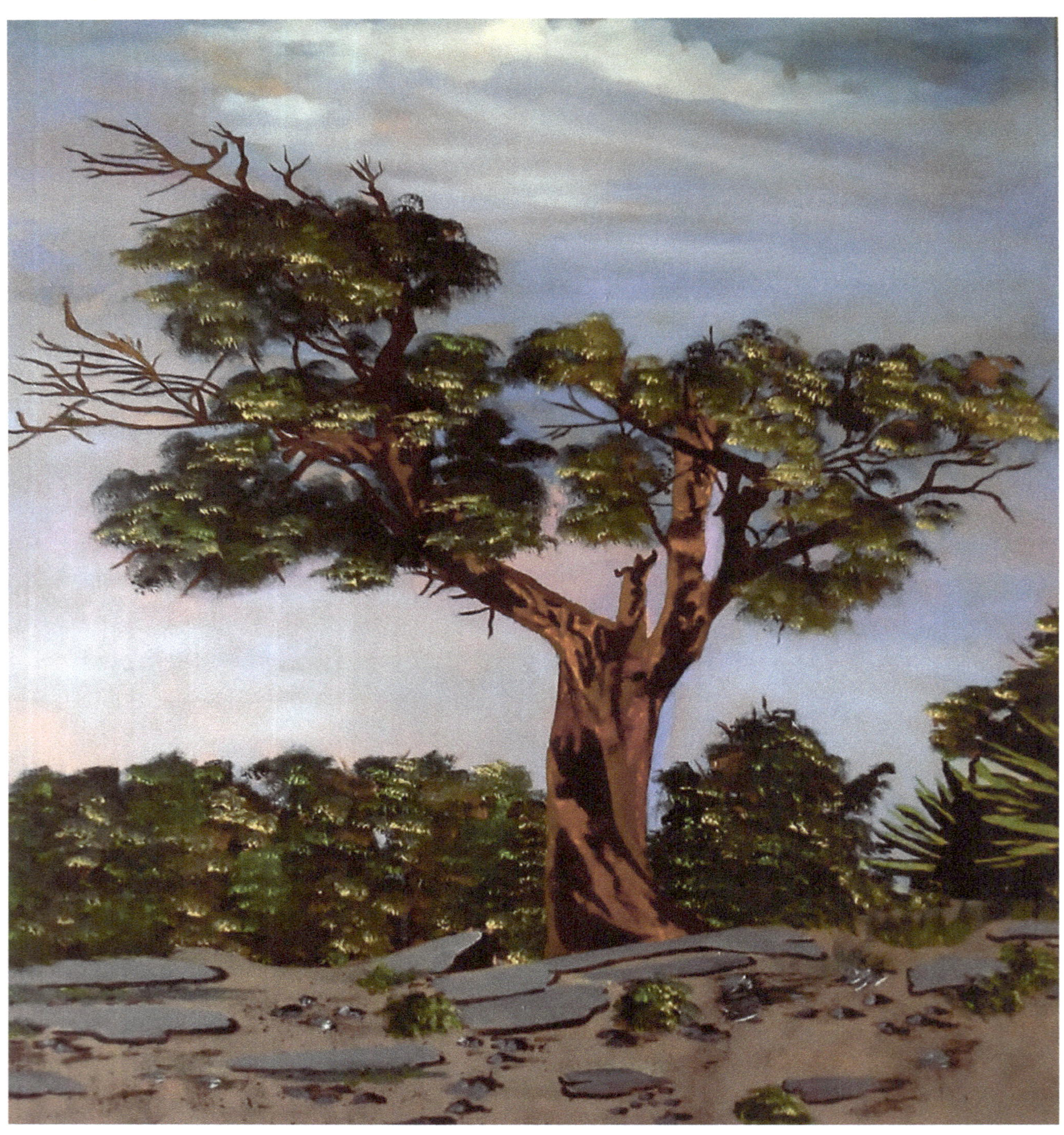

YOU'RE MAJASTY
16x20″
www.slikkersfineart.com

When a tree stands alone in the desert it looks so majestic. You stand in awe of the grandeur of the whole scene that god has created. The greatness of the branches and leaves make the sky so inviting. As you walk along the trail you imagine that the next step will bring spring desert flowers. They too are so awesome.

Please make a black and white picture of the tree and study the lights and darks that this method shows.

YOU'RE MAJASTY

Paints:

1. Burnt Sienna ½"	4. Cobalt Blue ½"	7. Black ¼"
2. Burnt Umber ½"	5. White 1"	8. Yellow Light ¼"
3. Raw Sienna ¼"	6. Payne's Gray ¼"	9. Sap Green ¼" Yellow Ocher

BRUSHES:

Cheep brush 1", sable ¼", sable ½" sable flat ¼" sable flat ½". #2 sable

PREPARING THE CANVAS:

Start with covering the canvas with the Luminous Orange and letting it dry. Now apply the drawing or trace the picture on canvas and proceed to painting with the flat black Acrylic covering the darkest areas with dark black and lighter areas with just brushing or dry brushing on the painting. Cover the canvas with Roberts's medium and cover it with paper towel and brush with the same 1" brush that you used to add the medium, do this until you have it dry enough to see the finger print on your finger

I always start a painting with going from the top to the bottom and from the back to the front. As I paint the sky I paint over the branches and will also paint into the existing tree and shrubs. This always allows the sky to drop behind the subject.

SKY: mix cobalt blue and white.

Start with the cobalt blue straight and then add a touch of white to make it darker in some areas. Add white to the blue to make a light blue. Do not paint the areas you left open for the clouds. If you look at the tree you notice that the tree leans or it appears to lean to the left. I painted the clouds in white having the same leaning motion, movement of wind. As you paint the clouds touch into the blue and use this color to add puffs in the clouds. I am sure by now that you have noticed that the blue of the sky seems to separate, this is how the pink shows through in some of my skies.

A. **SHRUBS AND PLANTS:** Green is the equal amount of Burnt Umber and Cobalt Blue. This will make your darkest green. When you pull the paint to one side and the color underneath is more brown then and some more blue. The dark green when pulled aside is more blue then add more brown until it shows a dark green.

B. Med Green: take some of the dark green mixture and add some white and a little blue to achieve this shade of green.

C. Light Green: Sap green and add some yellow light.

When you are painting the shrubs use the brush to tape on all of the darkest color first and come back using the next medium green to make all of the under shades and finish off the plants using the mixture for the light green. All of the plants will always use the three colors as basic. You may then use your own discretion to achieve the exact look you want. The cactus to your right on the painting uses a different smooth stroke instead of the tapping motion.

TREE: Paint the trunk and main branches first. All of the darkest holes and splits on the trunk will show dark so use the darkest of the browns, if you want them to be more extreme use some of the black mixed into the burnt umber. The other color to work on the tree is the burnt sienna and to highlight the tree use the yellow ocher. You have painted the shrubs next and into the tree trunk area so now paint over the plants and you have set your tree in front. At this point you may now add all of the stray branches and twigs using the dark brown mix.

LEAVES: This may sound like old hat by now but at this point you paint the clusters of leaves in the same manner as the shrubs dark green, medium green and finish with the Sap green and yellow green mixture.

STONES AND LAND: The sand in the desert has a light brown or more on the gray side of the color spectrum. The sand will be painted first mix some of the burnt umber with white and use an x stroke so that the land mass will have some holes that you can be creative with. Add sticks, plants, even little desert creatures that are hiding in the holes. Plant the big flat stones using the Payne's gray and underling the front sides of the stones in black indicating that the stones are thick. Please don't forget the little stones or pebbles, they also cast a shadow.

Go back and see if you learned anything new in this lesson. I found that painting this tree was not an exhausting feat, just something that let me relax and feel good and it sold as soon as it was finished.

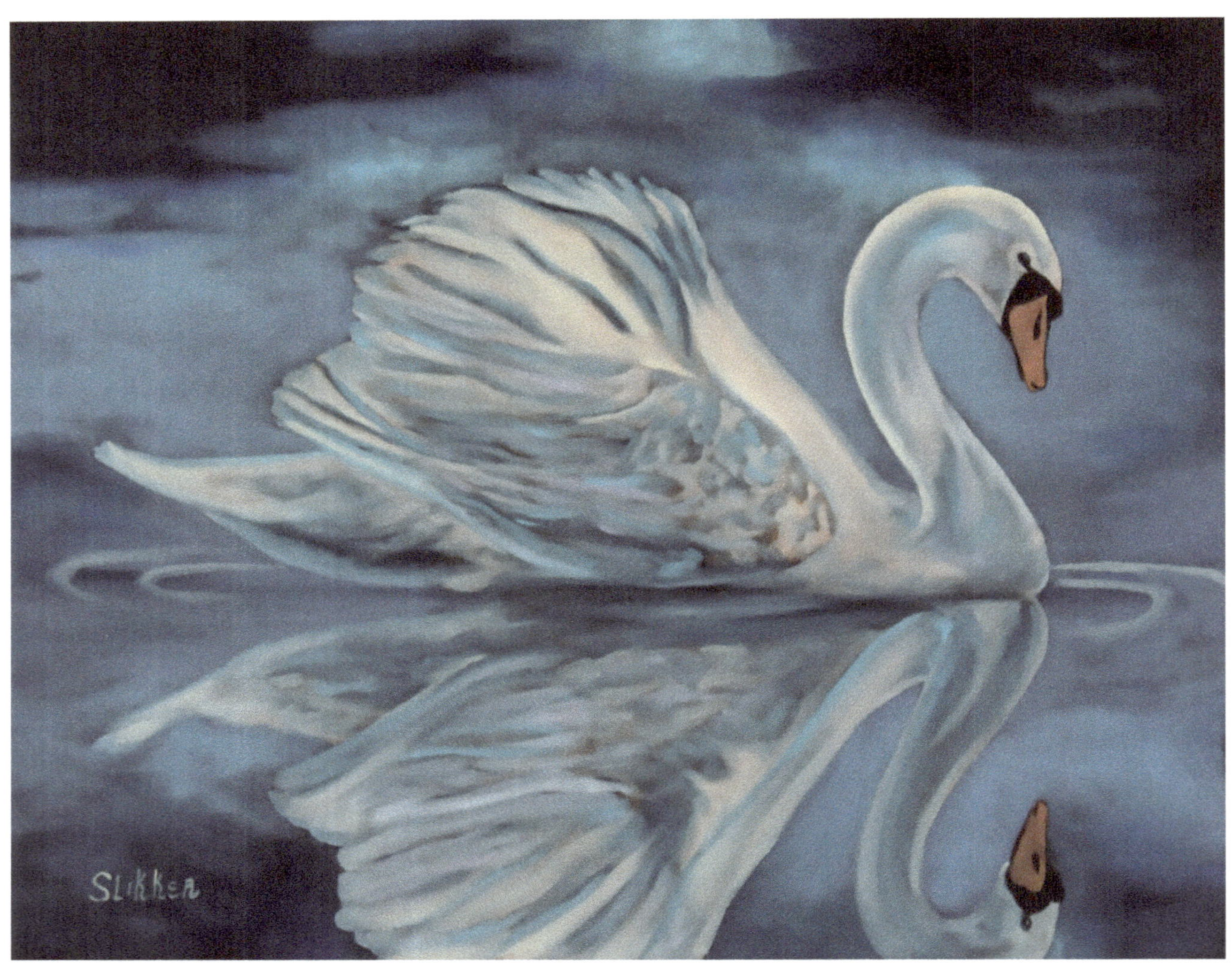

REFLECTIONS
18 ″X 20″

This painting of Reflections now has its home in Metropolitan Gallery Las Vegas Art Museum

www.mglv.org

CANVAS PREPERATION: Cover the canvas this time in flat black. Cover the canvas except paint around the swan. Use the black to put in the dark areas on the swans. All areas that show darks on the swan will be black, which include blues and lavender. You will now cover the entire canvas in Robert Warrens medium using the 1″ flat brush and then using a paper towel brush the towel until the painting is dry enough to leave the finger print showing.

PAINTS: violet, white, cobalt blue, red medium, cad. Yellow med., black, turquoise

BUSHES: 1″ cheap brush, ¼″ sable, ½″ sable, ½″ bristle brush, hake brush

Lavender: ½″ white, ½″ violet, touch of black touch, touch.

Orange: ¼″ red med., ½″yellow med. if it is too bright add some white

Blue: ½″ white and ¼″ blue

A. We will start with the water, using your black paint over the flat black leaving the area that you want to paint blue to enhance the swan. Please keep looking at the picture that you copied from the book.

B. **Swan:**

   Looking at the swan paint all of the dark areas with black and violet dropping down to the wings use lavender with some very dark violet at the base of the swan making the line of the water very flat and still. Now we will add the white of the swan while looking at the picture you must be careful to be putting the blue in the swan's neck to shape the area around the bill and make the neck curve. As you paint the body and wings and tail with the white, make sure that at this time blend into the black and violet shadows and shape of the feathers in the swan.

C. **BILL AND EYE:**

   Using black add the eye and the black around the bill. Using the orange mixture add the bill and with the black add the nostril in the bill.

D. **HIGHLIGHTS ON WATER:**

   I highlighted the water using some lavender around the forward part of the neck of the swan and where ever I felt I could use some more color the add interest on the painting. Using the blue mix add the water lines around the swans. Directly under the swan darken with black to make the flat line under and between the swan and reflection. To give more interest in the painting I added some white and turquoise in the shadow areas of the swan.

E. **SWAN REFLECTION:** Repeat the same process for the reflection of the swan

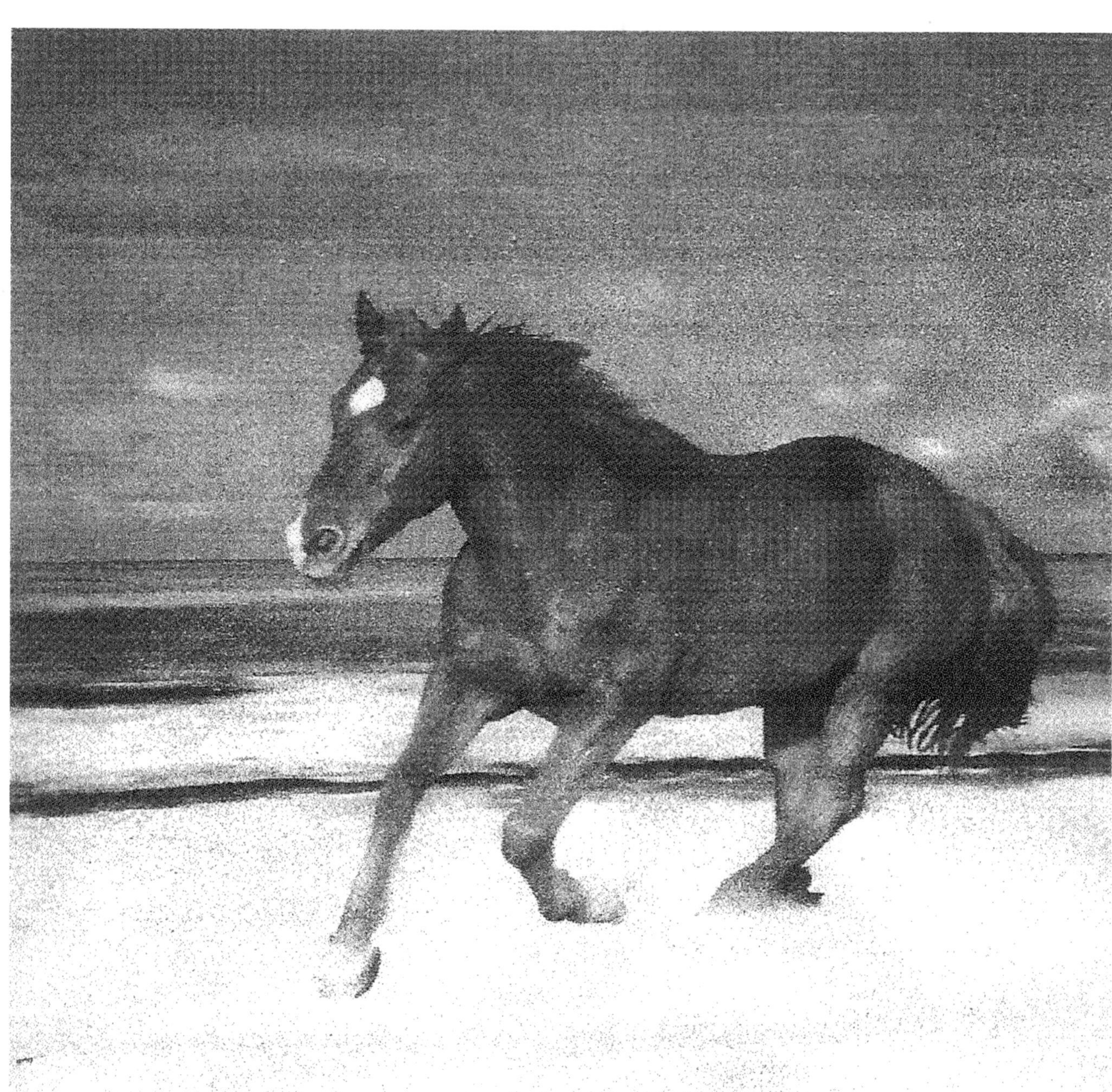

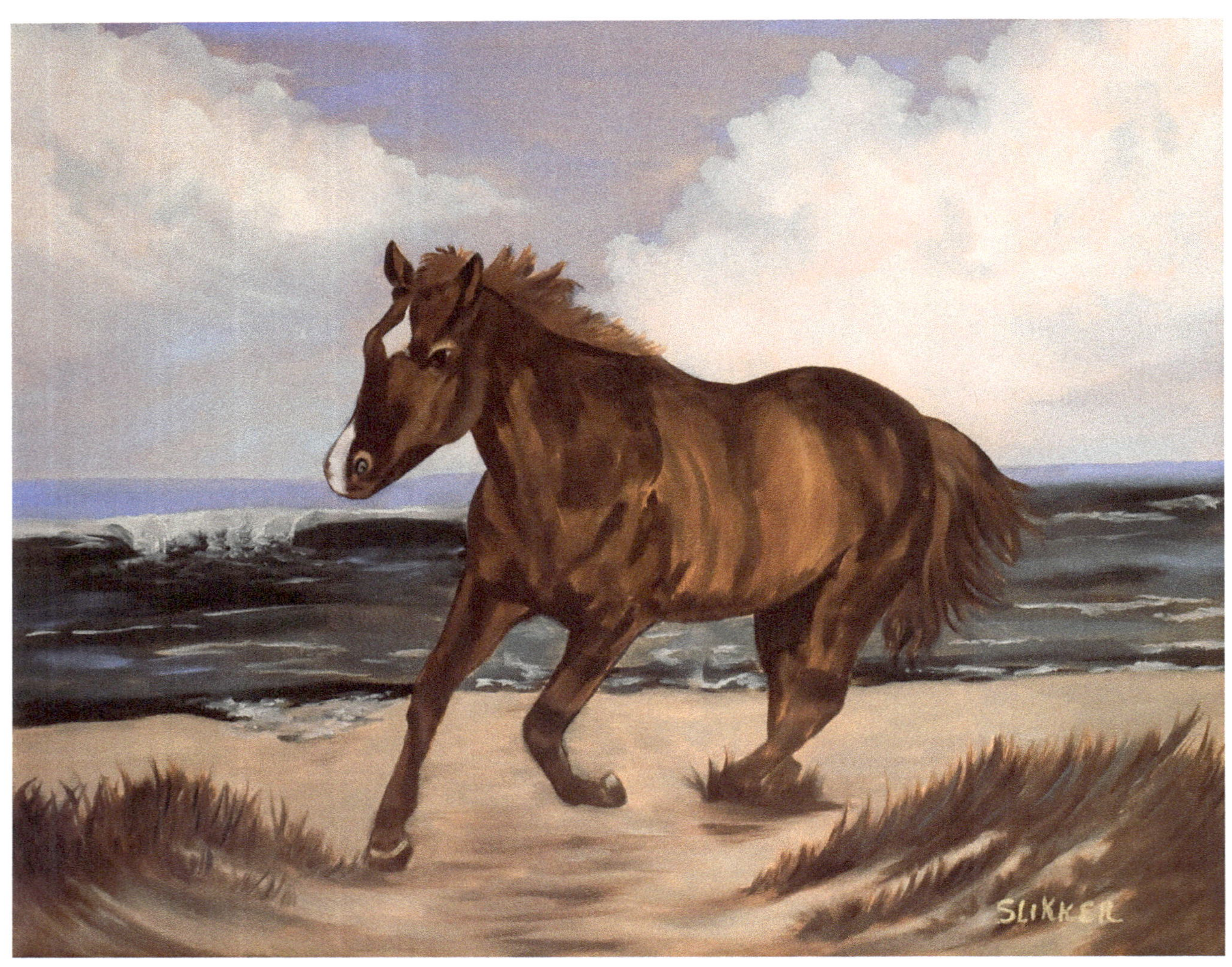

ROPER ON THE BEACH
16 ″X 20″
www.slikkersfineart.com

PAINTS: MARTIN F. WEBER OILS:
PRIMA OIL COLORS AND PERMALBA WHITE

1. Cobalt blue ¾″
2. Naples yellow ¼″
3. Cobalt violet ¼″
4. White 1 ½″
5. Peach ¼th″
6. Prima Gray ¼″
7. Burnt umber ½″
8. Burnt sienna ½″

Measure these out on your pallet straight from the tube. Slice the amount needed from the bead to mix your formulas for your colors. Number your pallet 1—6 to place the corresponding formulas.

Preparing the canvas: Luminous orange and flat black (acrylic paint)

Medium: Robert Warren's medium this will not yellow with age.

Brushes: 1″ Brush (to apply medium)

1. Scharff brush sable Filbert #6
2. Scharff brush sable filbert #12
3. Scharff brush sable filbert #2
4. Scharff bristle filbert #6 or #8

Color mixes:

1. **Lavender Blue:** ½″ white, ¼″ cobalt violet, ⅛″ cobalt blue
2. **Light Blue:** ½″ white and ⅛″ cobalt blue
3. **Cream:** ¼″ white and touch of Naples yellow
4. **Dark Green:** Equal parts of cobalt blue and burnt umber ¼″ of each
5. **Blue Green:** ⅛″ of blue green mix and ⅛″ light blue mix
6. **Brownish Gray:** Brush mix prima gray and burnt umber

"Roper on the Beach" instructions:

Paint the canvas with luminous orange, when it is dry apply the drawing or pattern.

Black work: follow the pattern that is all black; be careful to make it dark where it shows dark and brush lightly where it is light. After the black work is done apply a layer of medium, be sure to cover the whole canvas. Using a paper towel an 1″ brush, brush it dry (until you can see the lines of your finger print). To accomplish this use a dry paper towel over the medium, brushing until you have reached this point. (**please never use your hand to wipe the medium on the canvas to dry the medium. Only use the brush**)

#1 SKY: #10 Badger Filbert

A) **Lavender Blue mix #1**—paint 2″ down from top of canvas working around clouds.

B) **Light Blue mix #2**—Paint lower down to cloud profile and slightly under clouds to horizon. Add white to brush and ass lighter blue streaks to horizon working between bottoms of clouds and horizon. Blend into upper color using the X stroke.

#2 CLOUDS: # 10 Badger Filbert

A. **Cream mix #3**—Fill in light areas of clouds allowing some orange to show through.

B. **Lavender Blue mix #1**—Blot and stroke into shaded right sides of clouds working into cream for a lighter value. Add to bottoms of clouds and stretch out a few bottoms near horizon. Brush mix Lavender Blue and Dark Green and add a darker value to the bottoms of the upper clouds.

C. **Light Blue**—Blot into middle area of upward shapes as reflected light.

#3 WATER: (#10 Badger Filbert and mop)

A. **Lavender Blue mix#1**—Define horizon and fill approximately ½″ lower. (please note that the line of the horizon and water must be straight)

B. **Blue Green mix #5**—Blend and overlap Lavender Blue and fill in down to most distant crest. Paint lower area between crests (trough) blending over dark baselines of both close waves and blending up into translucent crest. Don't paint breaking foam areas of waves or flat surf lines coming up on sand.

C. **Dark Green mix #4**—Accent the dark base line of waves and blend into previous colors.

D. **Lavender Blue mix #1**—Add to the bottoms of breaking foam on waves and many horizontal movements to trough or flat areas. Add Prima Gray to brush and add a base color to thin surf foam coming onto sand.

E. **Light Blue mix # 2**—Add distant crest lines, close crest tops and front flat water movements.

F. **Cream mix #3**—Highlight tops of breaking foam sparkles to close and distant crest blending into lower Lavender Blue. Add a couple of foam edges to thin surf on sand using a straight edge of a palette knife with a small bead of cream. Press with downward pressure as you slide the knife edge back and forth.

G. **Mop water and sky**

#4. Sand (#10 Badger Filbert)

A. **Brownish Gray** Brush mix prima gray and a touch of burnt umber and cover the complete sand area.

    B. **Burn Umber**—Add to sand coming out of grasses. You will use this same color to place the grasses. Using a backward comma stroke you can form the slight hills that the grasses will be planted in.

    C. **Prima Peach**—Highlight the distant beach areas and the upward motion between the hill shadows.

    D. **White**—Add final accent to distant sand

#5. Horse (#4,#6, #2 filbert, #2 pointer, 3/8″ fur brush)

    A. **Burnt Sienna**—Completely cover the horse, except the markings of white, and the eyes.

    B. **Burnt Umber**—Using this color you can now go over all of the dark areas of the muscles.

    C. **White and Cream**—Using the cream fill in the markings and highlight with the white.

    D. **Naples Yellow and Cream**—Highlight the areas that are catching the light. Please refer to the photo.

#6. Mane and Tail (3/8″ fur brush)

    A. **Burnt Sienna and Burnt Umber**—Be sure to follow the shapes of the mane and tail. Use the side of the brush to place lines and the flat of the brush to fill in and create the curving flow of the mane and tail.

#7 Grasses:

    A. **Color #4**—Place the grass coming out of the brown clumps. This would be the time to add highlights on the grass if you wanted a different time of day. If you wanted sunlight then don't paint so many clouds and then highlight the grass with sap green and yellow.

Any time when you are using a lesson such as the one I have laid out for you, do as much as you can to make the painting your own by changing things that would work for the piece and also make it your own. Such as the landscape, what I started with was just a photo of my sister-law's horse and I chose to put it in the ocean scene. Have fun and let me know how things are going for you.

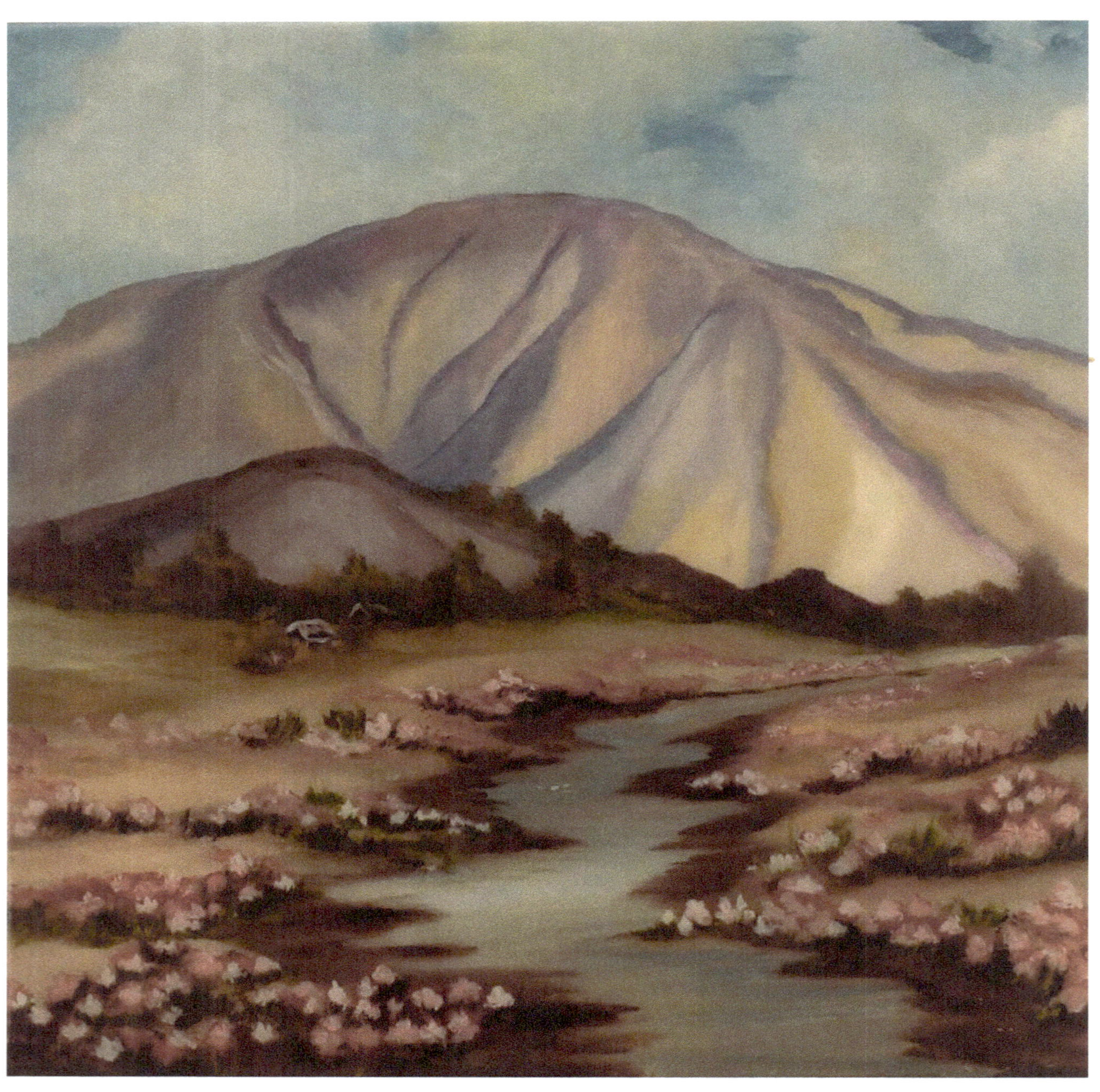

SPRING TIME ON THE DESERT FLOOR
11 ″X 14″
www.slikkersfineart.com

#1 Canvas Preparation:

A. Completely cover your canvas with Robert's Luminous Orange Acrylic paint and let dry completely.

B. Draw your mountains and stream with the flat black acrylic (black study) making the dark creases in the mountains dark and using the dry brushing technique for the lighter areas. Along the stream banks they will also be dark. Try to plan ahead where you want to plant the flowers leaving small holes in the black for flowers. This process is to make the flower brighter when they are painted. After you have finished the black study cover the complete canvas with Robert Warren's special medium making the complete canvas shine. Using a paper towel and using the same 1″ brush you used for the medium, lay the paper towel on the canvas and brush the paper towel until you have dried the medium just enough that when you touch it with your finger, you can see the finger print clearly.

COLORS USED:

A. White

B. Burnt Umber

C. Cobalt Blue

D. Burnt Sienna

E. Pink

F. Cobalt Violet

G. Sap Green

H. Cad. Yellow Light

I. Cad. Red Med.

J. Yellow Ocher

BRUSHES:

A. Cheap 1″ brush for applying medium

B. Sponge brush for applying Luminous Orange

C. Scharff sable ¼″

D. Scharff sable ½″

E. Scharff Bristle ½″

MIXTURE OF COLORS:

Dark purple gray—¼″ cobalt blue, ¼″ cad. med. red, touch of black, to lighten add some white.

A. Light Violet—¼″ violet, ½″ white

B. Pink—½″ pink and ½″ white

C. Dark Green—½″ cobalt blue, ½″ Burnt Umber

D. Yellow Green—¼″ sap green, ¼″ yellow light, some white

Painting the mountains:

A. Using the dark purple gray paint all the dark crevasses dark on all of the dark areas on the mountains.

B. Blend on out using the light violet (remember the dark to light rule)

C. Next use the yellow ocher mixing with some white to create the next light on the back mountain.

D. The smaller hill—Use the darks and put it in front of the back mountain. It will look flat if you do not change the values for the front hill. Keep thinking hill and use a rolling motion with the brush. Starting with the dark purple and brushing it on down the hill adding a lighter value of the same color until you come to the light in front of the hill

TREES:

1. Using dark green mixture start tapping the shape of the trees along the base of the hills and mountains.

2. Light Green mixture will add some dimension to the shapes. If needed you could add some blue and white to dark green and add this value before applying the light green

3. Use the Burnt Umber to make the small buildings in the background. Refer to photo before making houses so that you free hand the buildings and then plant them with some bushes.

STREAM:

1. Using your Burnt Umber paint your banks on both sides of the stream with a back and forth motion of the brush, as you come forward on the stream to the front of the canvas you could mix a little black to your mixture to make it look a little more moist.

2. Using a light blue add water to the stream bed. Next dip into the light pink to add shadows in the stream. White shadows for the sky as they also reflect to the stream.

DESERT FLOOR:

1. Drag out the colors used for the trees and forward hills to start the floor of the desert. All the time using your own version of the color mixtures to build the floor using the photo as your guide.

6. As you work your way forward with the lighter colors add some rocks Burnt Umber and black. Later highlighting them with the light pink or mix some white with the brown or black to make a real light value to accent with and give them some shape.

FLOWERS:

1. Using red make the flowers by painting a red spot where a flower is growing.

2. Now with the light pink proceed to making the petals of the flowers (this is where I use my backward coma stroke)

3. Highlight or make the petals curve by using a dark pink

4. Add greenery and make shadows under most of the plants especially the ones in front of painting

RULES FOR OUTSIDE PAINTING:

DISTANT HILLS:

1. **Most Distant Hill**—Lavender Blue ¼″ white, ¼″ cobalt violet, ¼″ cobalt blue

2. **2ⁿᵈ Distant Hill**—Purple Gray ⅛″ white, ¼″ cobalt violet, ⅛″ black

   Light Purple Gray″¼″ white, ⅛″ purple gray (used for most distant and high lighting of closest mountain.

SOIL:

COLORS USED

1. **Burnt Sienna**

2. **Yellow Ocher**

3. **Raw Sienna**

4. **Raw Umber White**

5. **Naples yellow**

TREES:

1. **Dark Green equal amounts of cobalt blue and burnt umber**

2. **Med Green equal amounts of cobalt blue and white with dark green mixture.**

3. **Yellow Green Sap green with white**

4. **Naples Yellow highlight trees and grasses**

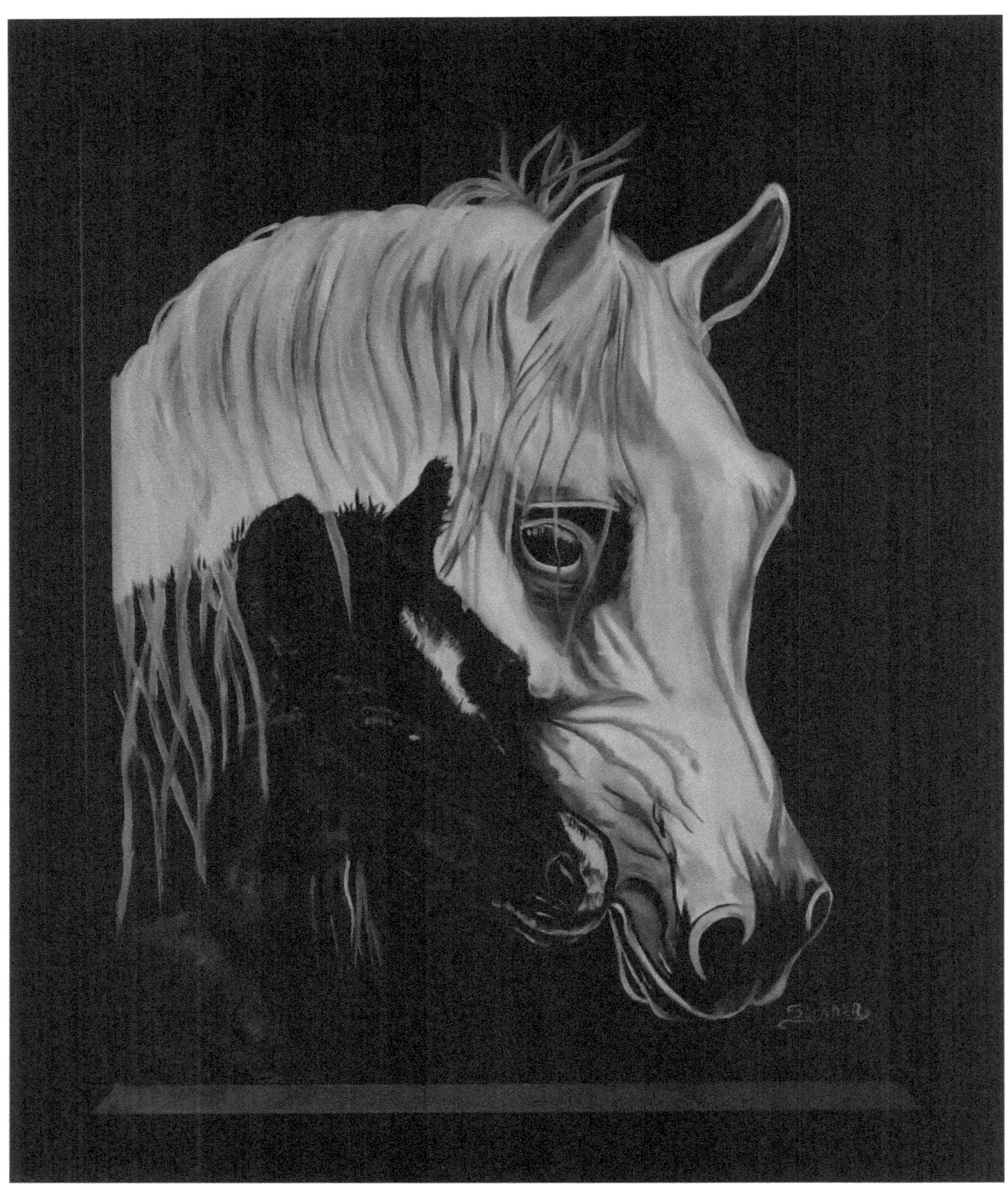

MOTHER AND CHILD
16 ″X 20″
www.slikkersfineart.com

The area that I live in here in the desert around Las Vegas, Nevada USA people have for their leisure and work a lot of horses. We are also loaded down with a lot of wild Mustangs. They roam the desert with their head of the household, the stallion; he is so proud of his family all of the Mares and foals. You will see him standing guard over his herd keeping his eyes open for danger of predators or other stallions trying to take over his family. As I was at the museum in Death Valley Junction I caught this family pose with my camera, came home to the studio and had to try to capture the love conveyed from mothers to their children, even in the animal kingdom.

I printed my photo in black and white to be able to see where my lights and darks would fall. Now it's time to begin.

CANVAS PREP:

This time I started by painting my canvas black up to my drawing. Over lapping the subject so that when I painted the portrait, the background would be in the back.

Using the black study I painted all of the darker areas with the black acrylic, dry brushing and painting lightly over the white horse. At the same time the black study was applied to the baby, only on the darkest areas.

With the sponge brush cover the canvas with Robert Warren's medium wetting all the areas. Now cover with paper towel and using the same 1″ cheap brush you used to add the medium now brush on the paper towel until you have dried the medium enough so that when you touch the canvas it shows your finger print clearly.

COLORS:

1. **WHITE**
2. **BLACK**
3. **BURNT UMBER**

MIXTURES:

1. ½″ white, ¼″ black making a gray mix both dark and light colors of gray
2. ¼″ burnt umber, touch of white making a lighter shade of brown

BACKGROUND:

1. Use black to cover all of the background painting into the lines of the horse.

WHITE HORSE AND BABY:

1. Use black to paint the inside of ears, eye and mussel of the horse. Now paint above the eye in black slowly converting the color to the dark gray and continue to paint around the eye and mussel. The mouth is also black.

2. Using the white paint the horses head coming back with the lighter gray to put in the creases and main of the horse. Always refer to the picture at all times.

BABY:

1. Paint the baby in black except for the white areas. Use the soft gray to accent the eye and some of the markings and mussels of the leg. Now accent the head in the brown lightened with some white to shape the head and also touch on the body and legs.
2. Add white to the markings and blend into the markings some light gray

FINISHING TOUCHES:

Go back to both horses and add the finishing touches (baby's mouth, nostril, eye lashes. Always refer to the photo.) When using the med gray for the baby and a lighter gray for the mother's mane paint with a loose curve for mane. Make sure that you add lines for the veins on the mature horses face. Using the light to dark helps to make the veins come forward; blending with your hake brush is very helpful to soften the mouth and nostrils.

The baby's face is not as smooth skin as the adult so add a few hairs around the markings and head.

At this time I would like to add a few drawings to show how you go about making some of the things that I have discussed in the paintings that I have shared with you to day. These drawings will help you to understand the construction of the clouds, trees, mountains, roads and buildings. What you do to achieve the depth perception in different scenes. There will be my personal contact information if you have trouble doing my lessons or a question that I have not brought to your attention but one that needs to be addressed. www.dorothy1966@gmail.com

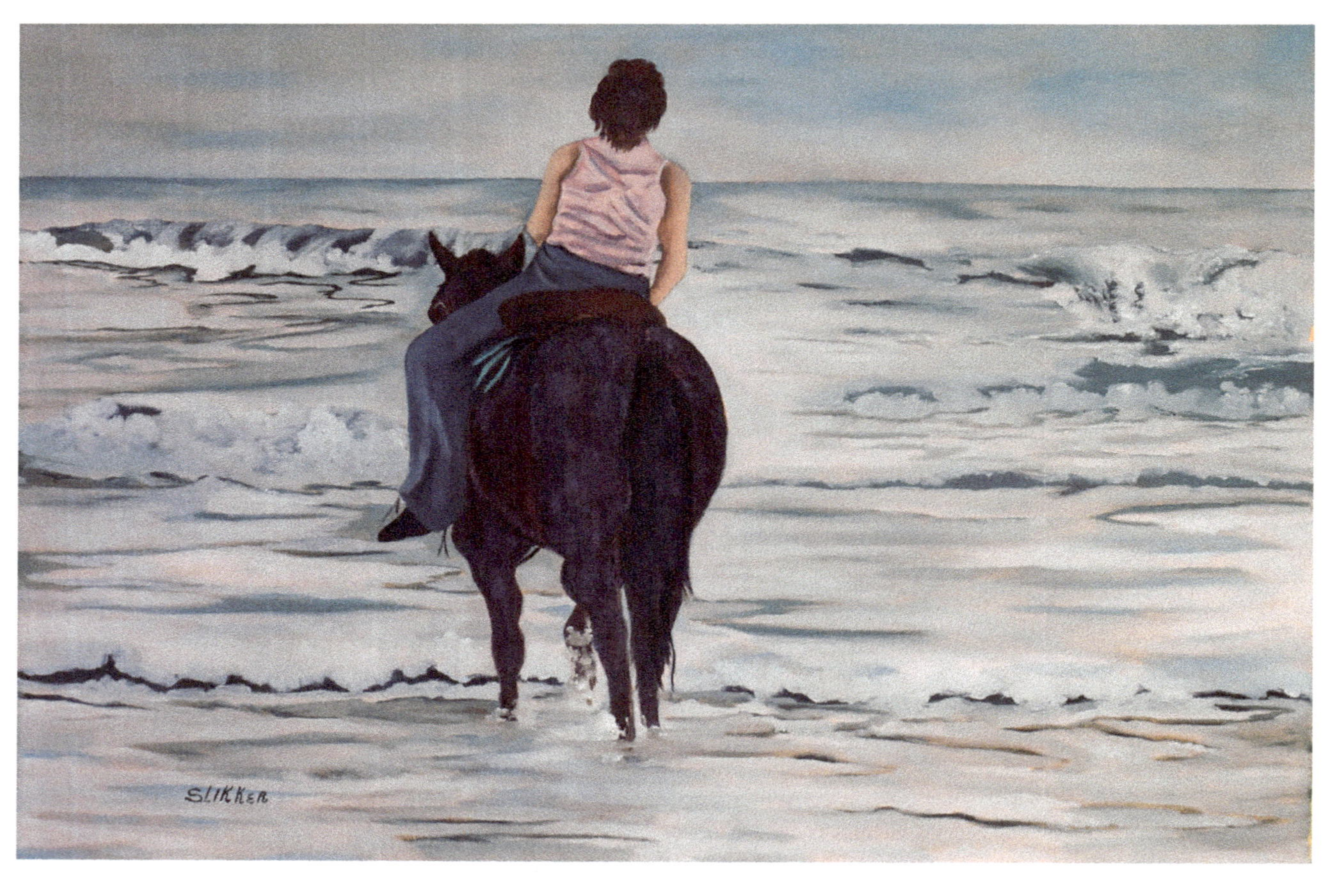

REFLECTING ON THE DAY
18 ″X 20″
www.slikkersfineart.com

We start by preparing our canvas with our Luminous Orange completely covering the canvas. We let it dry and then we apply our drawing or pattern allowing this step to dry (which takes very little time.) As you are doing the black study be sure to do the dark and lights with the wrinkles on the clothes, this will be helpful when you are painting the clothes on the girl. Also take care to do all the darks on the water as you need the darks to make foam.

PAINTS NEEDED:

1. **Cobalt blue**
2. **White**
3. **Burnt umber**
4. **Black**
5. **Pink**
6. **Burnt sienna**

BRUSHES:

1. Sponge brush (Luminous Orange)
2. 1″ cheap brush (medium)
3. ¼″ nylon brush ½″ nylon brush for applying black acrylic
4. ¼″ sable, ½″ sable #2 sable (Scharff) #6, or #8 sable

COLOR MIXES:

1. **Blue ¼″ and ½″ white = blue for water and sky**
2. **Equal amounts of Burnt Umber and cobalt blue = dark green for under and around water foam from waves.**
3. **Burnt sienna and white for light color on flesh and the dark areas on the flesh will be burnt sienna.**
4. **Dark green + white for blue green shade or second shade of green to make ocean water.**

As I have told you in the past I always start at the top working my way down and from the back to the front. Which means that I will always do the complete background first and painting into the subject so that the subject is always in front of the painting.

With that in mind let's do the sky. Apply blue randomly leaving areas to make clouds using white. Make them scattered just not grouping them in clumps, you can make them loose as I have chosen to do. The sky next to the water will always be the lightest part of the sky. Don't try to keep painting where the color wants to move just let the light shade of pink show through.

WATER: The water line at the horizon should be darker than the rest and the water line should be straight across the canvas. Use the dark green for the line and bring it on down with using the second shade of green, mixing this with the dark blue graduating into the lighter blue. Skip around the water and paint all the dark markings that you made when you did the black study using the dark green.

Making the wave use the dark green and the second green paint the crest of the wave and the falling of the wave. Using white now apply the foam. Remember to make the foam you must use the dark green at the under edge of the foam. Now graduate out into the water using the second green mix, white and light blue. Remember every crest or foam you want to show must have a dark under color. Using the blue give shape to different waves and crests, this ocean does not show beach area as the horse has walked into the water. Proceed on making sure that you work some dark into the water to cast shadow from the horse.

HORSE: Make sure that you paint all of the dark area of the horse using Burnt Umber and finishing off with Burnt Sienna. Make the mane and tail black.

JEANS: Using dark blue mixtures add a little black and paint the blue jeans. Accent the pockets with light and dark.

ARMS AND NECK: Using burnt sienna paint around the arm holes and down the arm, blending towards the outside. Now paint the part of the neck that shows. Burnt Sienna + white mixed to make a light shade that complements the dark part of the arm continue to paint the rest of the arm being careful to blend and make it smooth.

ROLL AND STRAP: While we are in the burnt umber use it to do the bed roll and strap on the horse. Use some white to make buckle on the strap. Use the blue to make fringe on the bed roll.

SHIRT: lighten the pink and proceed with the blouse. The rolls and creases will appear as you have already established them with the black study. You can accent the rolls by adding light pink or white to the top of the rolls.

HAIR: I used Burnt umber to comb into the hair, highlighting the hair with burnt sienna. If you want some lighter streaks in the hair you could use some yellow ocher or raw sienna.

SHOES: Paint the shoes black

Now go back and plant the hooves of the horse in water and make a wave splash on them.

Dorothy Slikker

ART TEACHER

One day my brother came over and had in hand every piece of equipment that you would have needed to paint your Bob Ross Master Piece. He said sister can you teach me how to paint. He possessed the desire and willingness to paint and learn. We set up shop and started on his project, he hung onto my every word and movement of the brush. That afternoon was a delight for me and it showed me that I had what it takes to give a meaningful class. Charles is gone now and I still have the memory that pushes me forward. Taking classes with some of Americas' best artist gave me the confidence to push forward and work with my Mentor Robert Warren and earning my certification gave me the momentum to move to the next step in teaching. I started with young children and taught adults at night. I then taught my first class at the Las Vegas Creative Painting Convention.

After entering contest after contest I won the honor of being in the TOP 60 INTERNATIONAL CONTEMPORARY MASTERS. At the same time of the year I entered another contest and was awarded the honor or being named one of the TOP 100 WORLD CONTEMPORARY MASTERS. With these honors I am pushing forward with this book to teach and paint with you all over the world.